CHAMPIONSHIP

TRACK AND FIELD

THE COACHES

F. X. CRETZMEYER
State University of Iowa

GEORGE T. EASTMENT
Manhattan College

JIM "JUMBO" ELLIOTT
Villanova University

GORDON FISHER
Indiana University

ED FLANAGAN
Boston University

BRUTUS HAMILTON
University of California

RALPH M. HIGGINS
Oklahoma State University

OLIVER JACKSON
Abilene Christian College

JIM KELLY
University of Minnesota

CLYDE LITTLEFIELD
University of Texas

JESS MORTENSEN
University of Southern California

LARRY SNYDER
Ohio State University

CHAMPIONSHIP

TRACK AND FIELD

By 12 Great Coaches

Written and Edited by
TOM ECKER

PRENTICE-HALL, INC., Englewood Cliffs, N.J.

PRINTED IN THE UNITED STATES OF AMERICA

12796—BC

DEDICATED

To all the friends of track and field who have made
this book possible, to my three children who have
made it necessary, and most of all, to the woman I
can't get along with, but would never be able to get
along without,

JUDY

Foreword

Introducing Tom Ecker to the readers of this book is a happy privilege, although it is no easy task to try to convey to you the sparkling variety of his personality.

Tom is, of course, a "track nut." But he is a rare and individual one to have conceived of and assembled this book while still in his middle twenties. This illustrates both his ability to dream up a brilliant idea and his persistence in pushing the inspiration to completion during months of disciplined work.

Tom's enthusiasm is infectious, too, as can be evidenced in the results of his three years of volunteer track and cross country coaching at Elizabethtown High School where he teaches math. Previously, the school had only a small track team, no cross country team—and it *still* has no track. But last spring the track team, and this fall the cross country team, were regional champions—the first two such championships ever won by the school in any sport—and one boy was state cross-country champion—the first state honor in the school's 60-year history.

This young man really gets around, too—geographically and with many people. He has been in every state except Hawaii. Much of the traveling was in a joint venture with his charming and talented wife (together they have composed a number of published and recorded songs) with an entertainment group they managed. Now his trips are mostly to the major track meets throughout the country, frequently with one or more of his boys along.

Of course into even such a sunny, active life some disappointments must come. When they do, they bring a shake of the head, a quick grin and gesture of hand, and he is reorganized to attack the revised or new objective.

As a high school athlete Tom won a number of individual state championships; at Iowa he was a member of championship relay teams at the Kansas and Drake Relays and was individual Big Ten champion at 600 yards in 1957. Swinging his arms high in his individual style he qualified, as a representative of our club, for the 400-meter hurdles at the National AAU Meet in 1959.

A charter member of our young Kentuckiana Cinder Club, Tom has contributed in many ways, for example, by organizing a decathlon to climax a series of Olympic Development Meets. It was a "first" for all twelve participants and for our area. But it moved on schedule and Judy (Mrs. Ecker) had complete point tables for every event, translating the points for the metric distances into the points for feet and inches, enabling us to give a cumulative score a few minutes after each event.

As his book goes to press, Tom is using his wide acquaintance and talents to excellent effect as coordinator of special events for the Mason-Dixon Games to be run on the unique eight-lap-to-the-mile board track in our Kentucky Fairgrounds Coliseum.

Starting our Kentuckiana Cinder Club from scratch three years ago has provided a continuing, heart-warming experience for many of us. It has renewed old and valued friendships as well as provided expanding opportunities to repay the debts we owe to track and field athletics. It has also brought fresh, new personalities into our lives and one of the best of these is the gifted producer of this book, Tom Ecker.

GEORGE G. GIBSON
Yale, 1925
President, Kentuckiana Cinder Club, 1957–

Louisville, Kentucky
January, 1961

Preface

In this one volume, *Championship Track and Field,* twelve of the most successful track coaches in America have collaborated in bringing their time-tested coaching methods to the coaches and athletes of this country.

The twelve contributors to this book have a total of 385 years experience in the coaching of track and field. Their athletes have won hundreds of national championships, 36 Olympic championships, and have held 89 world records.

Some of their phenomenal athletes include Rink Babka, Bob Backus, Ken Bantum, Greg Bell, Don Bowden, Don Bragg, Milt Campbell, Harold Connolly, Glenn Cunningham, Glenn Davis, Jack Davis, Ron Delaney, Aubrey Dooley, Charlie Dumas, Fred Dwyer, Bob Fitch, Fortune Gordien, Jim Graham, Al Hall, Sim Iness, Charley Jenkins, Deacon Jones, Lou Jones, Leamon King, Jim Lea, Dallas Long, J. W. Mashburn, Bobby Morrow, Tom Murphy, Parry O'Brien, Jesse Owens, Eddie Southern, Lon Spurrier, John Thomas, Max Truex, Bill Woodhouse, Mal Whitfield, Jack Yerman, Earl Young, and many, many others.

Nine of the 12 contributors to this book have coached United States teams in international competition and seven of those have had the honor of being U. S. Olympic coaches.

The material for this book was collected through a series of tape-recorded interviews with the twelve coaches. Traveling to and from these interviews carried me through one blizzard, one automobile accident, and 26 states. The first interview was held in a New York hotel. The final interview was held five months and 27,000 feet of tape later on a hillside terrace overlooking San Francisco Bay.

I am proud to be able to say that I have worked with all of these great men and that I was fortunate enough to have been coached by one of them.

ACKNOWLEDGMENTS

My thanks, first, to those who provided the excellent illustrations: John L. Griffith of *Athletic Journal,* Herman Masin of *Scholastic Coach,* Jay Simon, Ruth Ann Goranflo, and all 12 schools.

And of course I am deeply grateful to those who helped in the preparation of the manuscript, Judy Ecker and Richard Bell.

—Tom Ecker

Contents

CHAMPIONSHIP

TRACK AND FIELD

CHAPTER ONE

The Sprints

Oliver Jackson
Abilene Christian College

OLIVER JACKSON joined the Abilene Christian coaching staff in 1946, and since then has become known as an outstanding coach, lecturer, and goodwill ambassador.

Jackson is probably best known for his champion Wildcat sprinters, particularly Bobby Morrow and Bill Woodhouse. Morrow has best marks of: 100 yards, 9.3 (9.1w)* and 220 yards, 20.4 (20.0w). Woodhouse has run: 100 yards, 9.3 (9.1w) and 220 yards, 20.7 (19.9w). Jackson's sprint relay teams have tied or bettered world records five different times.

As a lecturer Jackson has instructed in track and field coaching clinics all over the United States. And in 1958, he and Morrow traveled the Caribbean countries on a six-week lecture and demonstration tour for the State Department.

Indicative of his standing in the track coaching profession, Jackson is President of the National Track Coaches Association, a member of the Association's six-man board, and a member of the NCAA Track and Field Rules Committee. For his work in track and field, Jackson was named to the Helms Foundation Hall of Fame in 1955.

* wind-aided.

The Sprints

Speed, strength, relaxation, nervous temperament, and age are all important factors in sprinting, but innate speed is definitely the most important. If a boy doesn't have natural speed, he can never become a champion sprinter. A boy's time in the 100-yard dash can be improved considerably by improving his start and his running form, but basic speed is inherited and cannot be improved through practice.

A boy must be physically strong in order to be a good sprinter. Sprinting is a strength exercise. More muscle strength is required for sprinting than for any of the longer races.

A sprinter has to be able to relax. Most great runners look as if they are loafing because they run so easily. Unless the ability to relax is acquired, a boy can never become a great sprinter—no matter how much natural speed he has.

Most good sprinters are the nervous, high-strung type although some control themselves much better than others. One of the things that made Bobby Morrow a great sprinter was his self-control. Within him was the nervousness that was needed to explode at the right time; yet he appeared as cool and calm as a two-miler. Because of that one factor, many sprinters actually froze in their blocks when they ran against Morrow during his greatest years. He had the necessary nervous energy inside, but outwardly he appeared calm and confident.

Age is more of a determining factor in sprinting than in other events. Sprinters do not usually excel for as many years as do distance runners. Many distance runners do well in their late 20's and early 30's, but most sprinters begin to fade at about age 25.

As far as size of the sprinter is concerned, there have been all types. Ira Murchison, who tied the world record for 100 meters, stood 5-4. Bobby Morrow, co-holder of the world 100-yards record, was 6-2. Dave Sime stood 6-3; Jesse Owens was 5-10 and Bill Woodhouse, 5-8. Size doesn't seem to matter at all.

The Start

Block placement. Our sprinters do not crowd the starting line nearly as much as some other sprinters. Although our sprinters get as close to the line as possible with their hands, their feet are behind, rather than under them. A boy doesn't have power to push forward if his feet are directly under him.

Block placement varies with the individual. To adjust the blocks to a particular boy, have him take the "set" position behind a starting line with his stronger foot against the front block. The block should be placed 16 to 21 inches back from the starting line, depending upon the length of the sprinter's leg. His hips should be two or three inches higher than his shoulders, and there should be enough forward lean so that his shoulders extend four inches ahead of his hands.

Then the back block is moved forward against the back foot until you find the "power points" on the blocks. These are the points where the sprinter feels he has maximum power to drive with both of his legs.

A sprinter uses both legs when driving out of the blocks. He pushes against the back block as well as the front block, although the thrust against the back block is not as great, naturally, because the boy's center of gravity is forward. As long as the back leg is limp, the block setting is wrong.

In the blocks. When our sprinters take their marks, they step in front of the starting line, drop down on their knees and back into the blocks. The number of arch injuries and foot and calf cramps is greatly lessened by having sprinters back into rather than step down into the blocks.

All of the spikes of each shoe should be placed firmly against the starting blocks. If the boy's toes are bent so that all of his spikes are not against the blocks, there will be a split second delay as he thrusts forward. There will be no lost motion as he drives forward, however, if he has backed firmly against the blocks with all of his spikes.

The sprinter's shoulders should be as high as possible when he takes his marks. His arms are locked straight, and he gets as high on his fingertips as possible. The hands are shoulder-width apart with thumbs turned in and fingers out.

As soon as the sprinter takes his marks, he relaxes and rocks forward so his shoulders are about four inches ahead of his hands. Then on the command, "Set," he raises his hips straight up.

In the set position the boy's hips should be only two or three inches higher than his shoulders. If the hips are too high, a great deal of the opening drive will be lost.

We try to keep the boys from thinking about the gun. Some coaches feel that sprinters should concentrate on the gun, but it is my feeling that they should be concentrating on power and drive from the blocks. If a boy is ready to run, any loud noise should cause him to respond. That's why it is so essential to keep the crowd quiet when sprinters go to their marks.

In the set position, the sprinter's eyes are focused only three or four yards down the track. Attempting to look farther ahead will cause tension in the neck and shoulders when the runner should be relaxed.

Driving from the blocks. One of Newton's laws of motion is: *For every action there is an equal and opposite reaction.* Thus, harmony must exist between the runner's arms and legs in order for him to be balanced and have maximum power. If one leg is thrust back against its block, the opposite leg must begin a forward thrust in order to keep the arms and legs coordinated and to prevent lateral rotation of the hips.

Many sprinters tend to "run through the hoop" formed by their arms as they come out of the blocks. In contrast with the vigorous, driving arm action which should be used, their arms form a hoop which they practically step through before arm action is begun. (See Figure 1.)

At the sound of the gun, the boy who starts with his left leg forward will drive momentarily against the back block with his right leg before his front leg begins its drive. Since there is an equal and opposite reaction for every action, it is natural, then, for his right arm to be thrust forward momentarily to compensate for the driving of the right leg against the back block. This forward movement of the right arm is only a few inches and is

FIG. 1

"**Running Through the Hoop.**" This is a common fault among sprinters. The arms form a hoop which is practically stepped through before arm action is begun. (Courtesy *Athletic Journal*)

barely noticeable, but it is important. A boy who does not develop this slight forward thrust will start out off balance and may run several strides before his arms and legs finally become coordinated.

Then comes a great thrust of the left arm as the sprinter takes his first step out of the blocks. The driving action of the left arm is out and up, and the right arm does the opposite. He should try to maintain the 90-degree angle of the arm throughout this action. (See Figure 2.)

The first stride should be as long as the boy can possibly carry it and still remain balanced. The longer the opening stride the better, up to a certain point. I think the idea of having a boy chop his first stride isn't sound. His first step should be long and as relaxed as possible and still be driving. Of course, a tall boy's opening stride will be longer than that of a shorter person.

The first step out of the blocks must not be off to the side. The beginning sprinter will often take a first step that is two, three, or four inches out of line when driving from the blocks. Then when he pushes with that foot to thrust himself forward, he is pushing laterally across the track as well as forward. Finally, after 10 yards or so, the boy is running in a straight line, but he has been running laterally, and any lateral motion takes time. Every motion should propel the body straight forward.

For the first 20 to 25 yards of the race, the sprinter leans forward with all of his power behind him. Probably the most disastrous fault of many sprinters is to jump up from the blocks instead of pushing out when the gun sounds. It is impossible to get any running power in an erect position. The sprinter should leave the blocks at less than a 45-degree angle as his legs try to catch up with

FIG. 2

The Start. Bobby Morrow of Abilene Christian College, winner of three gold medals in the 1956 Olympics, drives from the blocks. Notice Morrow's forward lead and the driving action of his arms. (*Courtesy Athletic Journal*)

the rest of his body, and should reach a sprinting angle of about 70 degrees at no less than 15 yards from the starting line. (See Figure 3.)

The Stride

In the 100-yard dash, the runner must maintain forward body-lean so the driving action of his legs will be behind him throughout the race. Forward lean is determined for the most part by the knee action of the runner. Correct knee action will bring about a good natural body-lean.

Proper knee action for sprinting is "up and out." As the knee is lifted up, the lower leg swings forward like a pendulum, reaching out for the ground. If the knees are lifted straight up, the sprinter will have little or no forward lean. If he does not lift his knees at all as he runs, he will do all of his running behind him and may stumble because of too much forward lean.

Since the dashman's stride is longer and more rapid than that of the distance runner, there has to be a longer, more vigorous swing of the arms as well. The sprinter vigorously works his arms; yet he must keep them relaxed as he runs.

Relaxation cannot be overemphasized as an important factor in sprinting. When a boy is running relaxed, he is running at his best. In fact, practically all the boys who break world records on the track have the ability to relax and make it look easy.

After he has run an especially fast race, it is not unusual to hear a boy say, "I didn't think I was running very fast at all. If I had given it a little more. . . ." But per-

FIG. 3 **Driving from the Blocks.** World record-holders Bill Woodhouse of Abilene Christian and Dave Sime of Duke reach a forward angle of 50—55 degrees 5 yards from the blocks. The sprinting angle (about 70 degrees) should be reached at no less than 15 yards from the starting line. (Courtesy *Scholastic Coach*)

haps if he had known it and had given it a little more, he might have tightened up and not have run as well. (Figure 4 shows Bobby Morrow easing up at the tape in a preliminary 100-yard dash heat at the 1957 NCAA Championships. His time was 9.3, tying the world record. Morrow's winning time in the finals was 9.4.)

To teach relaxation, we watch each boy's facial expression as he runs. When a person begins to tire or when his muscles tighten up, it shows in his face first. If the muscles of his cheeks and jaw are tight, he cannot be running relaxed. We jokingly tell our boys to let their eyelids bounce as they run. If their eyelids are bouncing, they know they are relaxed. Of course, the eyelids cannot really bounce, but we do watch to see if their cheeks are bouncing. If the cheeks are actually flopping, the runners are probably relaxing or at least trying to relax.

Our sprinters do a lot of running at ⅔ and ¾ speed to stress the importance of learning to relax. In the fall the boys even run cross-country to further improve their relaxation and endurance.

The Finish

If the runner thinks in terms of running through the tape rather than jumping for it, he will get to the finish line more quickly. (Figure 5 shows Bill Woodhouse running through the tape, tying the world 100-yard record of 9.3.) Nothing is gained by leaving the ground in order to break the tape. Speed is gained on the ground, not in the air.

Also, there is not nearly as much chance of a "finish line injury" if a sprinter keeps his balance at the finish of a

FIG. 4 **Relaxation.** Bobby Morrow is relaxed as he finishes a 100-yard heat in world record time. (United Press Photo)

race. In the 100-yard dash, many injuries occur from the 90- to the 105-yard mark. This is because so many sprinters lose their balance trying to lunge at the finish of a race rather than finishing with a driving rush at the tape.

Since tight races are often won or lost in the last two or three yards, any good sprinter should learn to lean into the finish line to get an extra few inches over his opponents. Through practice, boys can be taught to get an extreme lean in the last two or three yards of a race and still remain balanced. Lee Calhoun was probably the greatest "leaner" I have ever seen. He won the Olympic high hurdle title in 1956 when he outleaned Jack Davis and then won again in 1960 by outleaning Willie May.

The 220

In the 220-yard dash, the sprinter's feet are not as far behind his body as in the 100; his body lean is not as pronounced, and there is a slight decrease in the driving action of his legs. Some people call the running action in the 220 a "float." I think it is simply relaxation. The 220 man must drive hard for 15 to 25 yards and then relax but still carry that opening speed throughout the race.

As he comes off the turn, the sprinter can pick up speed by increasing the length of his stride. The only way a runner can increase length of stride is by lifting his knees higher in front, thus allowing his back leg to straighten out completely for that maximum forward thrust.

In training for the 220, more repetition work should be done than for the 100. Boys have to be much better conditioned to carry their top speed over the longer distance.

FIG. 5

The Finish. Bill Woodhouse drives for the tape on his way to a share of the world 100-yard record. (Photo: Abilene Christian College)

Workouts

During the fall months, all of our boys run cross-country—sprinters included. Over-distance work not only conditions and strengthens the body, but it also teaches boys the advantages of learning to relax. They must learn to relax in order to run long distances.

Workouts consist of three to six miles of cross-country running five days a week. They may fartlek (described in detail in Chapter 12) one day and do continuous running the next. Cross-country is a sort of game with our sprinters. They learn to enjoy it.

When track season begins, we like our sprinters to be a little overweight—and they usually are. A sprinter will lose weight by the second or third meet. If he continues to lose weight after that, he should probably be checked by a physician.

Our sprinters begin their workouts each day with 15 minutes of jogging on the grass. Loose jogging is the biggest part of our preliminary warmup. Any time the temperature is 70 degrees or above, they are required to do all of their jogging barefoot. This is done for two reasons. First, running barefoot on the grass toughens their feet. And second, it tends to massage the sciatic nerve in the arch of the foot. The sciatic nerve is the largest nerve in the body, running up the back of the leg into the small of the back, and connecting there with nerves that run out through the arms. The massaging of the sciatic nerve relaxes the entire upper body.

Calisthenics for sprinters consist of bending exercises primarily. No extreme hurdling stretches are allowed. Too much stretching, especially on short-muscled boys, may lead to knotting of muscles and eventual muscle pulls.

Our sprinters work hard. Besides their regular workouts, they often spend 15 to 20 minutes practicing baton exchanges, running as many as ten repeat 75-yard dashes while trying to improve their sprint relay baton passes.

Sprinters should seldom run against the watch during workouts. A watch is used during early season when we have the sprinters run 300's at a predetermined pace and when trying to perfect the first 50 yards of the race. A coach can convince his sprinters, by clocking them in short dashes, that they can better their over-all time with improvements in hip position, forward lean, and arm action out of the blocks.

Our sprinters never run against each other in practice. We try to build up each boy's belief in himself by keeping him away from competition with his teammates. If one sprinter is better than the others and they race too frequently in practice, the boys who do not win may build up a feeling of inferiority.

During the days when I had Griggs, Woodhouse, Segrest and Morrow, the four who broke the world record in the 440-yard relay (39.7), they seldom ran against each other in practice. Each boy should feel that he is as good as anybody else. If he doesn't have confidence in himself, he can never be a top sprinter. If he goes to the blocks feeling inferior, he is inferior.

Workout Program

Our training routine during mid-season for sprinters runs something like this:

MONDAY: 15 minutes of jogging on the grass.
                   15 minutes of calisthenics. Three repeats
                   on in-and-out 220's on the straight-away.
                   Form work on the blocks, but never at full
                   speed. Finish with a 220 on the curve at
                   ¾ effort.

TUESDAY: 15 minutes of jogging on the grass.
                   15 minutes of calisthenics. Five to six 75's
                   on the grass at ¾ to ⅞ speed. 10 to 12 starts
                   with the gun. Handle baton on sprint relay
                   exchanges for 15 minutes. Finish with a
                   150 at ⅞ speed.

WEDNESDAY: 15 minutes of jogging on the grass.
                   15 minutes of calisthenics. Two laps around
                   the track doing in-and-out 110's. Five or six
                   starts with the gun. Two 50-yard sprints at
                   near top speed. Handle the baton on relay
                   exchanges for 15 to 20 minutes, taking two
                   or three at top speed. Finish with easy
                   strides on the grass.

THURSDAY: 15 minutes of jogging on the grass.
                   15 minutes of calisthenics and easy stretch-
                   ing. Four or five easy starts off blocks con-
                   centrating on form. Handle the baton for
                   10 to 15 minutes at ⅔ speed. Finish up
                   with easy jogging on the grass.

FRIDAY: Very little other than easy stretching and
                   jogging on the grass. We do not like to get
                   on the track on Friday at all. When travel-
                   ing, we do not work out on Friday except
                   to walk and do some easy stretching.

SATURDAY: Competition.

Common Injuries

Among sprinters, muscle pulls are probably more common than any other type of injury. I don't think anyone in

the world knows exactly what causes pulled muscles or how they can be prevented.

Since warming up properly is commonly believed to be a preventive measure, the boys must warm up well before they run. But that doesn't always seem to be the answer. Recently, one of our boys pulled a muscle while running his third 220, striding along at ⅔ speed. Perhaps this type of injury has to do with each boy's physical make-up. Some boys may be more prone to muscle pulls than other.

Some sprinters develop arch or ankle trouble if they have been running on hard surfaces. A preventative is having them work out in short spikes. Often, long spikes and a hard running surface combine to cause a runner to have trouble with his feet and ankles.

Weight Training

Coaches and athletes are just beginning to scratch the surface of weight training. Although many new ideas are sure to develop, it is generally known that the day when a weakling can become a good sprinter is behind us. The boys who will win races in the future are the boys who are physically strong. Because of this, most coaches are beginning to have their athletes use resistance exercises in the form of barbells, dumbbells, weighted jackets, and leg weights. These give more resistance and thus increase muscle fiber strength. The only way muscle fiber can be strengthened is through resistance exercises.

For years athletes have been doing resistance exercises such as chinning exercises and pushups. Weight training is the same except that the resistance can be increased with an increase in weight. As long as we realize that sprinting is a strength exercise and we increase the resistance, boys will become stronger and will be better sprinters.

Beside our track is a weight-training room where all of our boys work with weights. They lift three days a week from the fall of the year until our season begins. Then they work with weights only two days a week—usually on Sunday afternoon and Tuesday.

The amount of weight that is used varies with the individual and with the exercise. Five- and 10-pound dumbbells are used for some of our arm exercises and up to 200 pounds for presses. (Weight training is described in detail in the Appendix.)

Because most runners tire in their arms, the arms must be strong in order to keep the full coordination between arms and legs. The arms play an important part in running. Arms determine how long the running stride is. The deeper the arm action the longer the stride; shallow arm action will shorten the stride. If strength in the arms can be maintained over the entire racing distance, whether it's 100 yards or two miles, the runner can maintain a smoother, more relaxed stride.

To strengthen arms, our runners do a lot of pushups. In fact we have two pushup machines that were built for us. They are actually two parallel bars 24 inches off the floor. We have two different widths—one for the larger boys and one for the smaller. Pushups are done in these pushup machines, which allow the chest to drop down considerably lower than with a regular pushup, causing the chest and shoulder muscles to really stretch.

Before the Meet

On the night before a meet, boys should get the same amount of sleep that they have been accustomed to. If they are used to nine hours sleep, they should sleep for nine hours. If they have been getting 11, they should get 11 hours of sleep.

A sprinter needs to know as much about his opponents as possible. We talk over the race with our sprinters, discussing the other runners' strengths and weaknesses and plan our race accordingly. If we are up against a boy who has a poor start and a fast finish, we know that our men will have to get such a lead on him that when the opponent sees our sprinters pulling away from him in the first 25 yards, he will begin to tighten up trying to catch them. Or an opponent might have a very fast start and we will plan to really work to stay with him for the first 25 yards.

Our sprinters come out on the track 45 minutes before race time to begin warming up, using about the same exercises they take before practice sessions. However, there are none of the hard resistance exercises such as pushups. The warmup consists mainly of jogging and stretching.

The boys lie down and rest for 10 minutes before the race. After they get up and jog for a few minutes, they are ready to go.

CHAPTER TWO

The Quarter Mile

JIM "JUMBO" ELLIOTT
Villanova University

JIM ELLIOTT has been track and cross-country coach at Villanova University since his graduation in 1935. As a competitor at Villanova, Elliott was one of the country's better quarter-milers. He pushed Charles Hornbostle to a new world indoor record and won all but one race during his three years of outdoor dual-meet competition.

Elliott has developed great teams over the years at Villanova. His 1957 team, probably the most famous, performed a feat unprecedented in collegiate track history by winning the National AAU and IC4A indoor titles and the IC4A and NCAA outdoor championships. For this accomplishment Elliott was named Track Coach of the Year by *Track and Field Newsletter* and by the Rockne Club of Kansas City.

The Penn Relays has been the greatest scene of triumph for Elliott's Wildcat teams. Three consecutive years his team copped the sprint medley, distance medley, and mile relay races, setting records in all three. His mile relay teams have won six straight victories.

Many individual stars have. blossomed under Elliott's guidance, too. Six of his pupils have competed in the Olympic games, bringing home four gold medals, while many more have won fame as national and eastern champions.

The Quarter Mile

My interest in the quarter mile began in Philadelphia where, as kids, we used to watch mile relay races at the Penn Relays. Mile relay running has been the basis of the Penn Relays since the meet's inception in 1895 when eight mile relay races made up the entire program. The Penn Relays has grown into the biggest relay carnival in the world, and from the mile relay races we watched there as kids has grown my fondness for the quarter mile.

Physical Qualifications

When picking out boys to run the quarter mile, look for those who have unusual sprinting ability, size and strength, and the ability to relax while running.

The first requirement of a quarter-miler is speed. Although the 440 was once considered a middle distance race, in modern days it has become a long sprint. Nowadays, the good quarter-miler drives out of the blocks like a sprinter and runs the entire race at near top speed, allowing himself only a brief period of relaxation before the gather and drive for the finish line.

Because speed has become so important, the quarter mile is now a sprinter's race. It is much easier to build up a sprinter's strength and endurance for running the quarter than it is to try to develop speed in a middle distance runner who may not have much sprinting ability to begin with. For this reason, many more sprinters convert to running the quarter mile than do half-milers.

In track, as in any other sport, a good big man is going to be better than a good little man. With a few rare exceptions, this is particularly true of the quarter mile.

Charlie Jenkins stood 6-1 and weighed 170 pounds when he won the 1956 Olympic 400-meter title at Melbourne. Ed Collymore, who might have been our greatest quarter-miler had he not been injured his senior year, was 6-1½ and weighed 175. One of the exceptions to the rule about size was George Guida, one of the best quarter-milers I ever coached. Although George was small, he was a member of the 1948 Olympic team, finishing sixth in the 400 meters.

But big or not, a quarter-miler must be strong as well as fast. Over-all strength is of the utmost importance in quarter-miling. A boy's legs must be strong to sprint for 440 yards. And when he is tiring in the last 40 yards of a race and his legs finally give out, the quarter-miler has to carry through and finish the race with the strength of his arms. The runner who is not physically strong will not succeed in this situation.

The other important quality of the successful quarter-miler is the ability to relax, using only those muscular actions which will contribute to the most effective running. Relaxation cuts down on muscle fatigue and allows the runner a stronger, better-controlled body throughout the race.

Running Form

The running form of a boy depends upon his individual walking characteristics, since the way a boy runs is closely related to the way he walks. Thus, a boy who has his own individual manner of walking will also have his own individual running form.

A boy's walking or running form depends upon his physical structure. Some will run with a higher arm carriage than others, some a higher leg kick-up in back, or a shorter stride, or possibly a more exaggerated arm swing. The runner's style is his own, and as long as he remains relaxed as he runs, it is the best running form for him.

All that we really stress in our workouts is relaxation. It may sound elementary, but relaxation is the greatest word in track. At Villanova, we go in for a lot of relaxed running at $9/10$ speed. A runner who relaxes and runs at $9/10$ speed without pushing will run as fast, if not faster, than if he had tried to drive hard all the way.

To aid relaxation, look for the little things the boys do that keep them from being completely relaxed. Often, by having the runner lower his shoulders a half inch and drop his chin slightly, he can relax more as he runs. Or, subconsciously he may be clenching his fists, thus tightening up his arms and shoulders. By keeping his wrists loose, the runner's hands will automatically relax.

Relaxation is largely mental effort on the part of the runner. He has to concentrate on relaxation until it becomes part of his running form. Jenkins, for example, ran with ease because he learned to run relaxed. His stride and arm action were smooth and effortless as he ran. (See Figure 6.)

A few running "errors" that many young runners make can be corrected through relaxation, but, unfortunately, too few high school coaches attempt to correct the bad running habits that young boys develop. When boys reach adolescence, they go through a clumsy period, picking up

FIG. 6 **The Quarter-Mile Stride.** Charlie Jenkins of Villanova, 1956 Olympic 400-meter champion, illustrates his smooth, effortless stride and arm action. (Courtesy *Scholastic Coach*)

peculiar walking and running habits. In fact, at the teen-age level we've found that, in general, girls have better running form than boys.

At the college level we do not attempt to make changes in a boy's basic running form, although we do try to correct any bad habits that might slow him down. For example, we correct a boy who gallops by showing him how to relax and drive equally with both legs. So that he can gain better traction, we teach a boy to toe in slightly. And, of course, we don't want a boy to throw one arm out to the side as he runs. No one would run with one leg flying out to the side, so why throw an arm out there?

Another mistake often made is encouraging quarter-milers to take a longer stride. In early season practice it's all right to have them take long strides occasionally to increase hip flotation, but telling a boy to stretch out in order to increase the length of his running stride is ridiculous. The boy must run within himself. Overstriding in a race brings about fatigue much more quickly than if the runner is using the stride that is best suited to his physical make-up.

Attitude

You have to sell quarter-milers on a program of hard work. The only way they can become great runners is by living track 11 months a year, 24 hours a day. How they live and what they do during that time determines the degree of greatness they achieve.

Since the coach is with his team for only an hour and a half every day, a great amount of the responsibility of training lies with the boys themselves during the 22½ hours when they're on their own. The importance of hard work has to be planted in the runners' minds so that they realize that becoming great is entirely up to them. They must be shown that there is no shortcut to success and that only through hard work can a quarter-miler achieve greatness. If they are convinced of this, they will have the proper attitude for achieving that greatness.

Of course, just having the proper attitude isn't a sure road to greatness, but it definitely is a requisite. There are hundreds of examples that will bear this out.

Pre-Season Training

During the fall, our quarter-milers jog a mile before practice and a mile after. Their warmup includes all of the general over-all calisthenics that are common to trackmen, particularly the hurdle stretches for loosening of the crotch and hips. Before workouts, we do the calisthenics that stretch muscles rather than those that build muscles. As for artificial warming or loosening of muscles through rub-downs, we don't do it. A good trackman doesn't need a rubdown unless he has an injury; then it may help.

Our runners work five days a week during the fall. The quarter-milers are allowed to run on the cross-country course on two of those days if they like, but for three days a week they are required to work on the track where we can see them. We work them pretty hard and soon can tell which boys are progressing and just how they'll do during the indoor season.

We like to work our quarter-milers in progressions. We run repeat 220's, concentrating on relaxation not speed, hitting them in about 28 seconds. Or we may run repeat straight-aways, jogging the curves between them. It's amazing how much can be built into a runner. At first they can do only five or six 220's, but they build up to where they are able to run 13 or 14 of them.

During our workouts, we are actually concentrating on two things. We teach our runners the little things that aid in their relaxation, and we give them the work they need to increase their stamina, strength and speed.

Weight Training

My assistant, Jim Tuppeny, takes care of the weight program. He makes sure our quarter-milers go through an extensive weight-training program beginning in the fall. Rather than trying to build any particular muscles, he stresses general body-building.

When the boys begin, they do a lot of repeats in series of fives with full extension and contraction of the various muscles. Three days a week are spent in the weight room, but never is any heavy lifting done.

Then, in January, the weight training tapers off to one day a week. By May, work with the weights is completed for the season, but if a boy has any noticeable weaknesses at that time, he is instructed to begin work on the particular weaknesses the following fall.

To further develop the runners' arms, which are especially important when finishing a race, we have them hold bowling pins in their hands and practice running in place in front of a mirror every day. This helps develop the powerful arm action that is so necessary in the quarter mile. In addition to the bowling pin exercises, arms are further developed through pushups.

Season Training

When working with quarter-milers, we have found that the easiest thing to do is GET them in shape. The hardest thing to do is KEEP them in shape.

By the time the season rolls around, weight-lifting tapers off almost completely, although pushups and other arm-building exercises are continued throughout the season. When warming up for workouts, the boys continue with the stretching exercises that will loosen the crotch and hips.

Work has to be given in spurts. Our boys work hard at the beginning of the week and taper off from there. Their toughest workouts are on Monday and Tuesday, followed by two easy days, a day of rest, and Saturday's meet.

A typical week might go as follows. Monday's workout would consist of repeat 660's. On Tuesday we would run 300's back to back, jogging a lap between them. Wednesday's workout would be a lot easier—straight-aways and baton passes. On Thursdays we always take it easy, jogging and doing easy exercises, and rest on Friday for Saturday's competition.

Since boys are not all alike physically, some can work harder than others. You'll have to reprimand some because they're not working hard enough, but care must be taken so that you do not give any runners too much work. The coach must learn to recognize boys who are not progressing well and their need for more or less work. You must strive to improve each boy at his own rate.

Some boys want to be great so badly that they push themselves too hard. A coach has to be very alert and make sure that overanxious runners don't overwork themselves.

Pre-Meet Psychology

In track, the coach has to keep everything as simple as possible, and the boys have to be able to think for themselves. Prior to a meet, the coach should talk to a boy only if he has something constructive to convey. A lot of idle talk preceding meet after meet isn't effective. A runner only wants and needs to hear the things that will help him to run a better race.

We have special meetings with our boys only four times during the season. Those four meetings are held prior to our most important meets and are the only occasions during the season when we bring our boys up before competition. At those times we usually get a little extra effort from some of the boys. The rest of the time we say nothing and let the boys think for themselves.

Occasionally, a boy will become unduly nervous before a meet. Of course, some nervousness is necessary for a top performance, but too much nervousness can be harmful. We try to convince him to forget about the race. We tell him, "After all, of all the people in the stands there are only four or five who worry about whether you do well or not—your parents, maybe a girlfriend, yourself, and myself. What's the sense in worrying about it?"

Warming Up

Warming up, like so many other phases of track and field, is an individual thing. Every trackman has a "ritual" he goes through when warming up. What our quarter-milers do and how they do it is up to them, although I do like to see them begin warming up about an hour before race-time.

To begin, they usually jog a little, following that with the same stretching exercises that they use in practice. After about a half hour of warmup, the boys stretch out and relax until time for their race. When the weather is particularly cold, more warming up is necessary, and of course, less is required when it is warmer than usual.

The Race

The quarter-miler must drive out of the blocks like a sprinter. How far he drives is an individual matter, depending upon how long it takes him to build up his momentum.

In order to turn in the best possible 440 time, the quarter-miler's first 220 has to be fast. Our biggest problem with Charlie Jenkins was in getting him to run the first half of the race at top speed. He felt he had a terrific kick and could loaf the first 220, saving himself for the stretch run. But his best races were those in which he turned in a fast first 220.

Between the opening burst from the blocks and the final gather and drive for the finish line, there must be a period of relaxation. The runner will not become fatigued nearly so rapidly if he can maintain his relaxed running form at about $\frac{9}{10}$ speed throughout most of the race.

Curve-running is very important to the quarter-miler. A great deal of time should be spent in teaching quarter-milers to run the turns properly. They must learn to lean into the turns and run relaxed.

When finishing a quarter mile, the runner drives with his arms and holds his running form as long as he can. By the time he reaches the final stretch, his legs are completely "shot" and he must use the strength in his arms to help him maintain his speed throughout the final yards of the race. He keeps his chin down during the drive and runs through, not to, the finish line.

CHAPTER THREE

The Half Mile

GEORGE T. EASTMENT
Manhattan College

GEORGE T. EASTMENT was named head track coach at Manhattan College in 1946, after having compiled an amazing record as a high school coach at Bishop Loughlin in New York City. His schoolboy teams won six out of seven national championships and sixteen consecutive Catholic school indoor and outdoor titles.

At Manhattan, Eastment's teams have dominated track and field in the East. In the IC4A, they have won five indoor, four outdoor, and two cross-country titles. In addition, Manhattan has won more championships in the Penn Relays than any other two colleges combined.

Eastment has developed a number of outstanding athletes at Manhattan, including his two great half-milers, Tom Murphy (1:46.7) and Arthur Evans (1:47.9). Five of his track and field performers have been on U. S. Olympic teams.

In 1960, Eastment was one of the four coaches of the U. S. Olympic team in Rome. Two years before, he was head coach of the track team that represented the United States in a dual meet with the Soviet Union in Moscow. The American team, under his guidance, easily outscored the Russians.

The Half Mile

In recent years great improvements have been made in half-mile times, largely because the half mile is no longer a distance runner's race. Present day half-milers are boys who would have been running the quarter mile just a few years ago. All of today's great half-milers are fine quarter-milers as well. For example, Tom Courtney of Fordham, the 1956 Olympic 800 meters champion, won the National AAU 400 meters in 45.5, and Tom Murphy of Manhattan, the 1959 Pan-American Games 800 meters champion, was able to run a 440 in less than 47 seconds. In today's competition, the half-miler is a quarter-miler with the ability to carry speed over distance.

Physical Qualifications

There are no definite size requirements for half-milers. Top flight middle-distance men have ranged in size from 5-8 to 6-2 and from 135 to 190 pounds. However, they have all possessed speed and stamina, have learned to relax, and have been able to run the race smoothly while maintaining proper pace. A boy with a quick pickup will have a great advantage in competition in making tactical moves, such as getting out of pockets and passing opponents. This is especially true in indoor running where there are crowded fields, short straight-aways, and sharp turns.

Over-all strength is also important to the half-miler. If the runner has a weakness in any part of his body, it will show up in competition. To help develop strength, all of our runners do some weight-lifting, but never to see how much they can lift at any one time. Instead they do many fast repetitions with light weights. (See Appendix A.)

Running Form

In any event of track and field, there should be no set form. A coach who would adopt any particular style and make every athlete comply with that style would, in my opinion, be making a serious mistake. A boy's running style is inherited and usually is the best style for him. The coach should endeavor to smooth out the rough spots, see that the athlete is not doing anything contrary to the law of body mechanics, and let nature take its course.

It is elemental that extreme over-striding and under-striding are serious running faults. Of the two, over-striding is certainly the more serious. Many prominent coaches and outstanding athletes contend that a high percentage of American runners over-stride as they run.

Neither the runner's height nor the length of his legs determines the size of his stride. Both Arnie Sowell and John Woodruff, Pittsburgh's great Olympic middle-distance runners, had exceptionally long strides despite a difference of five inches in their height. On the other hand, Ron Delaney of Villanova, who was six feet tall, had one of the shortest strides of any outstanding runner in my memory.

Woodruff and Delaney, both Olympic gold medal winners, represented a great contrast in length of running stride. A study of pictures of these two athletes shows that both were bringing their lead leg down directly under the body despite the great difference in their length of stride. Based upon their height, weight, and general physical structure, they were able to achieve maximum efficiency.

Arm carriage is important to any runner, but again I believe nature provides the basis for the best form. The most important part played by the arms is at the finish of a race. Then the runner can drive with his arms to help propel himself to the finish line. If he can make his arms go, his legs will go, too, since it is physically impossible to make arms and legs work at different rates of speed.

When the runner's arms are bent at right angles to his body, he has the basis of proper arm carriage. Give or take a few degrees, this seems to be the ideal position for slow-speed running, with the arms moving straight forward and backward. Then as the pace increases, the arms are brought straight up in front of and almost parallel to the body. The arms must not be rigid and should break slightly from the elbow on the downward motion.

Workouts

In the fall, our half-milers run cross-country but, with only a few exceptions, they are not members of our cross-country teams. Our competitions in the East are over five-mile courses and are usually too long for middle-distance men. The entire cross-country season is devoted to building up strength and stamina—not to seeing how fast they can run.

To eliminate some of the monotony of fall workouts and to check on each man's progress, the half-milers report to the track twice a week to run "in-and-outs." Interval training, which I refer to as "in-and-outs," is repeat running

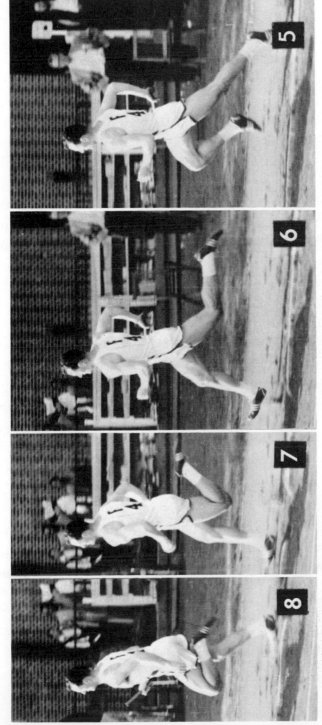

FIG. 7   **The Half-Mile Stride.** Tom Murphy of Manhattan College, 1959 National AAU and Pan-American Games 800-meter champion and 1960 Olympic team member, anchors the Manhattan two-mile relay team at the Penn Relays. (Courtesy *Scholastic Coach*)

done according to a planned schedule. The paces to be run and the length of rest between them are worked out in advance. In our workouts, interval training consists primarily of repeat 220's, 300's, and 440's.

How many repeats the athlete can do depends upon how fast each one is run and the length of interval between them. The coach may decide that the half-milers should run 220's in 28 seconds, but the question is "How much interval is there going to be?" A good runner, if given five minutes' rest between each 220, could run them for hours.

In interval training, the interval is as important as the time that is run. At the beginning of the year the runners are able to do only a few repeats and the interval of rest between them is long. As the season progresses and the athletes become better conditioned, the number of repeats that they do increases and the interval shortens.

"In-and-out" 220's can be made far more interesting by setting up relay teams in practice with five to nine boys on each team and having them run endless relays with the last man passing off to the first. If each boy averages 30 seconds for his leg of the relay, there will be a two to four minute interval between 220's. As the season progresses and the boys begin to run their 220's faster, the interval will automatically be shortened. The relay ends when the coach decides the boys have had enough.

Another excellent system of training is fartlek. (Described in detail in Chapter 12.) This always forms the basis of the first two months of our training.

Regardless of the day's workout, our runners spend not less than 30 minutes warming up before each practice. They begin by doing light jogging, followed by bending and stretching exercises. They conclude their warmup with three to six straight-aways (150's), with the first one at half speed and every succeeding one run gradually faster, but none of them ever run at top speed.

Many runners like to have rubdowns both before and after practice and competition. I am uncertain as to the need of rubdowns from a purely physical standpoint, but unquestionably they are worthwhile in aiding relaxation. Rubdowns relieve the physical and mental tensions that are built up in many athletes during practice and in competition. Where a competent trainer is available, the matter of rubdowns is best left in his hands.

Our half-milers do no over-distance work beyond an occasional three-quarters of a mile after our indoor season begins in mid-December. Along with most coaches, I feel that middle-distance runners should concentrate on speed. A runner needs over-distance work to condition himself mentally more than he needs it physically. If a half-miler can run a respectable three-quarters once every two weeks, he will not worry about his ability to finish in the half mile.

A common weakness among all runners, including half-milers, is the inability to judge pace, and the only way to overcome this weakness is by working under the watch.

Each boy should be given the time of every effort he makes so he will become pace-conscious and will know the difference between 56 and 58 seconds. If I would say to Murphy, "Let's run four quarters hitting them in 58, 56, 54, and 52," he would not miss any of them by more than two-tenths of a second. But that ability to judge pace was built up over a number of years. In order to develop skill in any phase of running, the athlete must work hard to develop that skill.

The coach should work out a training program that is

flexible enough to include the needs of each individual
runner. He should avoid as much as possible making a
hard and fast rule such as "Today all half-milers will run
interval 300's" because there will be some on the squad
who would be better off doing something else. Every boy
is different and what is good for one is not always good for
another. It is essential that each athlete be treated as an
individual, not only in regard to his running ability, but
in every aspect of his development. No two coaching situations are exactly alike. A good coach is one who can keep
an open mind and adapt to new and different situations.
The program should also be flexible enough to be easily
changed for a boy who improves more than has been expected as well as for those who are not doing as well as
expected. Until we have learned a great deal about our
young men as a result of our practice sessions and competitions, we cannot hope to set a definite program.

Every practice is concluded with three to six 150's, at
three-quarter speed as part of "warming down." This is a
good time for the coach to correct errors in running form
because they are much more noticeable when the athlete
is tired.

Training outdoors during the winter months poses a real
challenge in many sections of the country. In areas where
the indoor season begins in December, such as in the East,
rain, snow, and sub-zero temperatures make it necessary
for the coach to adjust his workout schedules to fit the
weather conditions.

To many coaches, getting ready for major meets in January would mean an entirely different routine from concentrating on reaching a peak for the championship meets
in May and June. Some coaches contend that it is impos-

sible for athletes to be at a peak over an extended period of time, but the trend in recent years has been to stay in shape the year round and "peak" for the "big ones." Each meet during the early season is its own test of one's condition. It not only acts as a guide in determining future workouts, but also brings the athlete a step nearer to his best performance at the end of the year when the championships are usually held.

Rest

I feel that nine hours of sleep is an absolute minimum for any athlete, and for a young boy it should be 10. No boy can succeed by working hard unless his body has time to build itself up again. If he works hard without sufficient rest, he will not progress in athletics and may endanger his health.

Foreign runners who work out two and three times a day make certain they get plenty of rest. At our international clinic at Berkeley, California, in 1956, I talked with a foreign coach who told me about a European team's daily schedule. They got up at six o'clock: They ran, they massaged, they ate, they slept. One o'clock: They ran, they showered, they massaged, they ate, they slept. Seven o'clock: They ran, they massaged, they ate, they slept. Without that rest those athletes could not possibly have kept up such a rigorous schedule.

The Race

There must be a relationship between the individual fourths of a race, whether it is each 110 of a quarter, each

220 of a half mile, or each 440 of a mile. Ideally, the four
220's of a half mile should be evenly paced, but it doesn't
always work out that way, any more than it did with the
four-minute mile. We think of a perfect mile in four 60-
second quarters; yet when Roger Bannister ran the first
four-minute mile, his quarter times were 57.5, 60.7, 62.3,
and 58.9.

Whether the 220's of a half mile are all even depends
largely upon the individual runner. Some runners are not
pace-setters. Tom Murphy and Jerry Siebert often ran
behind whatever pace was set and ran races with quarters
of 56 and 53, whereas Ernie Cunliffe often ran 53 or better
for his first quarter and 56 for his second.

Everything else being equal, the runner with a big "lift"
at the finish of a race will emerge the victor. Recent champions, such as Ron Delaney, Jerry Siebert, Tom Murphy,
and Tom Courtney, rarely, if ever, set the pace but instead
relied on a strong finish for their success. Arnie Sowell of
Pittsburgh, one of the all-time great half-milers, could run
it either way. He was usually the pace-setter, but whether
he was in front or behind, his smooth and seemingly effortless stride always left him with a burst of speed as he
neared the finish line.

If a boy does not have a strong finishing kick, his coach
should give him the type of work that will help him develop a better pickup at the end of a race. Occasional
slow-fast workouts may be used. For example, the athlete
may run an 880 with the first quarter in 65, the 660 in
1:38, and the last 220 all out. Of course, these fractions
would vary with the ability of the athlete. Workouts in
which a number of straight-aways are run at ¾ to ⁹⁄₁₀

speed with concentration on smoothness will help immeasurably.

Before the Meet

Too little sleep, as noted before, can be most detrimental to the runner, but getting too much sleep is often just as harmful. An extra amount of sleep the night before a meet will usually make the athlete sluggish and will keep him from performing at his best.

Trying to catch up on lost sleep the night before a meet is like eating a well-balanced meal the day of a race when eating habits have not been good prior to that time. One meal or one night's sleep cannot be expected to make up for weeks or months of poor training habits.

In the morning, I rout all of the boys out at eight to eat breakfast and go for a walk. They may return later for additional rest, but they must not lie around all day. Athletes tend to get sluggish if they are allowed to spend too much time lying in bed the day of a meet.

Most athletes should eat at least four hours before competition. Of course some don't need that much time to let their food digest but some need even longer. I once coached an intercollegiate 100-and-220 champion who ate a three-quarter pound steak an hour and a half before running. On the other hand, another sprinter I coached, who was the indoor intercollegiate and AAU champion, ate nothing for 24 hours before competition except tea and toast.

Warming up before competition is exactly the same as before practice. The athlete begins with easy jogging in his flats, followed by his bending and stretching exercises. Then he puts on his spikes and does his straight-aways (150's). The first one is slow and the others become progressively faster so the athlete will build his body temperature and loosen his muscles gradually.

Most boys need a pat on the back not only before a race, but also afterwards—win or lose. If a boy has run two minutes, he should be encouraged to try for 1:59. Every runner should have three goals; one for this week, one for this season, and the ultimate goal, but he should never have a goal that is completely beyond his ability. The winner may have earned a word of praise, but he must not be allowed to rest on his laurels. The loser, if he is to develop, is the one who most needs the words of encouragement. The right word from a coach, after a bitter defeat, may help today's also-ran become the champion of tomorrow.

CHAPTER FOUR

The Distance Races

BRUTUS HAMILTON
University of California

BRUTUS HAMILTON, three-time Olympic coach, is one of the deans of American track and field coaching. From 1924 to 1929, Hamilton guided Westminster College to five Missouri College Championships. In 1929 he moved to the University of Kansas, where in three years he developed two world record holders—Glenn Cunningham, one of the all-time great U. S. milers, and Jim Bausch, the 1932 Olympic decathlon champion.

Since 1932, when he moved to his present position at the University of California, Hamilton has developed a number of track and field champions and world record holders. One of his prize pupils, Don Bowden, was the first American to run the mile in less than four minutes.

Hamilton's name has been known internationally for many years. He was a member of the U. S. coaching staff at both the 1932 and 1936 Olympics and was head coach of the 1952 Olympic team at Helsinki. He has also coached American teams in Norway (1949) and Israel (1953).

As an undergraduate at the University of Missouri, Hamilton was an all-around athlete. He represented the United States in the 1920 Olympic Games Decathlon and Pentathlon.

The Distance Races

A spectator might think that boys are foolish to get out and run long distances. Actually, one should envy distance runners instead of feeling sorry for them because they usually are a happy group of boys. A young English poet once said ". . . we run because we like it, through the broad, bright land." * And all of our distance runners do like to run. One of the strange ironies of this strange life is that those who work the hardest, who sacrifice the most and achieve a goal, are the happiest of men.

Physical Characteristics

It has been said that it takes a lean man for a long race. Herb Elliot, the 1960 Olympic 1500-meter champion, was tall and lean, as were America's first four-minute milers, Don Bowden and Dyrol Burleson.

Most distance runners are lean, but of course there are exceptions. Jim Beatty and Max Truex, the U.S.A.'s top 1960 Olympic qualifiers in the 5000 and 10,000 meter runs, were both short and rather squatty. Beatty was the taller of the two at 5-6. Glenn Cunningham, the great distance runner from Kansas, was not exactly lean either. He stood 5-10 and weighed 155 pounds when he was competing. Emil Zatopek of Czechoslovakia, winner of

---

* From *The Song of the Ungirt Runners* by Charles Hamilton Sorley (1895-1915).

four Olympic gold medals in distance races, was short, thick-chested, and had rather heavy legs.

So distance runners do not necessarily have to be tall and lean. They can come in almost any size or shape as long as they are healthy and have the desire to run.

Most of today's top distance runners are fairly fast in shorter races, too, but not all of them. There have been some great miles run by men who were comparatively slow as far as sprinting ability is concerned. Merv Lincoln of Australia, for example, was a boy who had very little inherent speed, but built himself up to where he ran the mile in less than four minutes on several different occasions. I don't think he could have run a quarter in less than 53 seconds; yet he was apt to throw a 55 or 56 quarter at his opponents in the last lap of a mile.

The distance runner does not have to be tall and lean and does not have to have great natural speed, but he must have a good pair of legs, good lungs, and a strong heart, plus great enthusiasm for running.

Running Form

As long as a boy runs relaxed and easy, without any undue strain, his form is probably all right. Among the great distance runners you will see many different running styles. The form has to be suited to the individual. It is very much like the music teacher who was asked what technique she used in teaching her pupils. She answered, "I have 25 pupils. I use 25 different techniques." As long as the runner is running relaxed and has an easy, natural stride, I don't worry about his running form.

There are two barometers that indicate whether a boy

is running relaxed or not. One is his jaw. The jaw should be kept loose. The other is the fingers. The runner's hands may be open or clenched, but they should not be tense. The fingers must be relaxed.

The runner's arms must be relaxed and loose, too, swinging along for balance. Arm action is not vigorous in the distance races until the runner begins his home stretch drive.

The Mile

The mile run is a glamour event. It is an event where not only physical condition but tactics and mental attitude mean so much. The boys have time in four laps to rate themselves, to ration their energy, and to try to outsmart opponents.

Theoretically, the best way to ration one's energy over four laps is with four rather evenly paced quarters. However, my boys have always run the second half of a mile a little faster than the first half. I tell them to stay in contention during the first half mile, run as fast or nearly as fast as the other men, and conserve energy. Then as they pass the half-mile mark, they say to themselves, "Well now, that's over. It's just a half-mile race from now on." By running a moderate first half, the milers are able to save energy for the homestretch. That's where most distance races are won.

Milers seem to divide themselves into two classes. There is the "scientist" class, which is made up of runners who run scientifically, pacing themselves evenly. Paavo Nurmi, a ruthless adherent to the stopwatch, would have to be put in the scientist classification.

And then there is the "artist" type who depends more on inspiration and native speed to win races for him. The artistic runner runs against his opponents rather than against the stopwatch.

Nothing is quite as dramatic as a race between a scientific runner and an artistic runner—like the great duels between Glenn Cunningham and Bill Bonthron. Cunningham was the scientist and Bonthron the artist.

The casual spectator would ask, "Why doesn't Cunningham go out faster and take the kick out of Bonthron?" Or of Bonthron they would ask, "Why don't you just stay with Cunningham and outkick him?" Some days, try as he might, Cunningham just couldn't shake Bonthron, and other days, try as *he* might, Bonthron couldn't stay with Cunningham.

Each of these boys won several important races, although, I think, eventually more honors went to Cunningham. When Cunningham set the world record of 4:06.8 in 1934, he beat Bonthron handily. In the NCAA meet a week later, Bonthron stayed with Cunningham and outkicked him to win in 4:08 and a fraction. (Figure 8 shows Cunningham leading Jack Lovelock of New Zealand in a mile race. Lovelock, like Bonthron, was an artistic-type runner. He beat Cunningham in the 1936 Olympic 1500-meter race when he turned in a blistering 56-second final lap.)

There have been great milers who could combine both the scientific and artistic patterns. Herb Elliot was one. He could run fast in front, he could run from behind. A champion miler can either set the pace or follow. In coaching my boys, I tell them to try to be scientists for three laps and artists the last lap.

The Longer Distances (Two miles to 10,000 meters)

In the longer races, all of the quarter-mile times should be kept fairly even. Emil Zatopek, the great Czech runner who won the 5000 meters, 10,000 meters, and Marathon in the 1952 Olympics, ran with very little variation in his 440 times. He would step up the pace for the first 220, but then settle into his pace. All of his succeeding quarters would be fairly evenly paced except for the final lap, which was the fastest.

In training for the longer races, runners have to do much more distance work and a little less speed work. Work should be increased as the season progresses.

Racing Tactics

The tactical part of distance racing is very important. It is always wise for a boy who has a good kick to try to slow down the pace and then sprint in at the finish. A boy who does not have a very fast finish, if he knows others in the race can outkick him, has to go out and set a fast pace.

Many coaches tell their runners when they pass, to sprint past and take the heart out of an opponent. I tell my boys to ease by and not use sudden bursts of speed at any time during the race except at the finish line. A sudden burst of speed expends more energy than constant running, so it just isn't good economics to use much energy all at once until the end of the race where the race is going to be won.

When being passed, our runners hold their own pace and are not influenced by the pace of an opponent. The one

FIG. 8 The Mile Stride. Glenn Cunningham of Kansas University, world record-holder in the mile, leads New Zealand's Jack Lovelock, 1936 Olympic 1500-meter champion. (Courtesy *Scholastic Coach*)

danger in being passed is the tendency on the part of some runners to tie up. We try to protect against this tensing up by constant practice on keeping rhythm and staying relaxed. During the practice sessions we have the runner work on keeping his rhythm as a teammate sprints past him.

Workouts

When the boys come out for practice, they begin their warmup by trotting three or four laps on the grass and taking the regular stretching exercises. Then they do a little more running and are ready for the day's assignment.

In the fall, our distance runners work hard in cross-country. We do not emphasize cross-country as much as many schools in peaking the boys for certain races, but we do use it as a foundation for our work in the spring.

We do a lot of work on pace. Poor judgment of pace is a common weakness among distance runners. Often a boy will misjudge his pace and go out too fast the first quarter. If a runner can learn to pace himself correctly for the first lap, the rest of the race will usually take care of itself.

When Don Bowden ran his four-minute mile (3:58.7),* he took the lead at the beginning of the race and paced himself perfectly throughout. He kept clipping off 30-second 220's and then stepped up the pace on the last lap.

Our basic workout is the slow-fast. For example, when Bowden was in good shape, he would run a series of half miles slow-fast. He would run 60 seconds for the first lap

---

* At that time, only John Landy and Jim Bailey of Australia had ever run faster.

and 58 for the second. He could easily run three or four slow-fast halves in an afternoon.

All of our work is designed so the boys will run a strong final lap. Our workouts end with speedwork, either straight-aways or fast quarters. To develop a strong finish, we emphasize speed to all of our distance runners.

We have only one training rule at the University of California and that is to lead a normal, healthy life without excesses of any kind. So far this has worked very well. The boys want to do well, so they don't overdo anything—including their training.

Before the Meet

The coach has to get his boys into condition both physically and mentally to run the race. We often have a squad meeting the day before a meet to talk over opponents, discuss their strengths and weaknesses, and try to plan the race in advance, insofar as it is possible. We don't try to outline some mysterious strategy to outsmart an opponent. A boy who does that usually ends up by outsmarting himself. We just want each boy to run his own race, to keep his rhythm, to ration his energy, and to try to get to the finish line first.

Warming up before the race differs from warming up in practice. Some boys need a long, easy warmup; some need only a short one. One runner may take several fast bursts after his preliminary warmup. Another may only need to trot around, loosen up a bit, and take one quick burst to be ready. Each boy has to experiment to find out what is best for him.

Prior to the race, I give the boys advice but not a pep

FIG. 9   **Glenn Cunningham of Kansas and Don Bowden of California**—Two of Coach Hamilton's great milers. (Photos: Kansas University [left] and University of California [right])

talk. We discuss opponents and I make suggestions, but once the race begins, they are on their own. I don't believe a coach should be down on the field yelling at his boys. It is best to give a boy instructions and trust him to follow them through. Seldom have I been disappointed in expecting the best of my boys.

To cool off after a race, the boys trot around and "warm down," as they call it. They visit with their friends for a while and then go take a shower.

Distance Running in America

The United States is not as good in the distance races as many other countries, but it is not because American coaches lack knowledge of how to coach these events. I think it is because most American boys quit running as soon as they are graduated from college. At this age most of them are just beginning to run well.

Life is complicated for the American boy in his early and mid-twenties. He has both the service and his career to think about, so he doesn't have much time for running or training.

The peak age for distance running is usually between 24 and 32. Bowden ran the mile in less than four minutes when he was only 20; yet like so many American boys, he gave up running before he reached what might have been his peak age.

If by some chance we could change our cultural and economic pattern so our boys could have more leisure time, we would have great distance runners—men who could run with the rest of the world.

CHAPTER FIVE

The Hurdles

LARRY SNYDER
Ohio State University

LARRY SNYDER has coached a number of great hurdlers at Ohio State, including Dick Rockaway, Jack Keller, and Jesse Owens, consecutive holders of the world record for the low hurdles. Glenn Davis, the great all-around Buckeye trackman, still holds the world record for 400-meter hurdles.

During his undergraduate days at Ohio State, Snyder himself was an outstanding athlete, setting university records in the high and low hurdles, the high jump, and the broad jump. He was captain of the track team both his junior and senior years and upon graduation was awarded the Big Ten medal for combined excellence in scholastic achievement and athletics.

A member of the Ohio State coaching staff since his graduation in 1925, Snyder has gained world-wide recognition in track. His OSU athletes won gold medals in the 1936; 1948; 1952; 1956, and 1960 Olympics. He was a member of the U. S. Olympic coaching staff in 1952 and was head coach of the 1960 U. S. Olympic team. For his outstanding contributions to track and field, Snyder's name is permanently written on the Helms Foundation Hall of Fame Scroll.

The Hurdles

B oys like to jump over objects while running and they like to land running. As a kid, before I ever knew what a hurdle was, I would run along the street, jumping over bushes and signs, leaping off one foot and landing on the other.

To me, the hurdle events are the greatest of all track events. When a coach develops a boy who has the speed, strength, and agility to hurdle well, then he has a boy who can do a lot of other things, too. The boy can probably broad jump, high jump, and run on the mile relay team. When a coach develops a good hurdler, he has a boy who will really help the team.

Physical Qualifications for the High Hurdles

Hurdling was once an event left to those who weren't fast enough for the sprint events, but who were loose and agile. Years ago a high hurdler needed only good technique to win races, but now he must combine his ability to get back to the ground quickly with fine running speed. Speed has become absolutely imperative in the hurdle races.

Of course, agility is still a requisite for running the high hurdles. It is almost impossible to make a high-grade hurdler out of a boy who is tight in the hips. A lack of flexibility will cause the hurdler to twist his body as he goes over the hurdle and land off balance. Although looseness in the hips is not natural to some boys, it can be developed with stretching exercises.

The taller a boy is, the better chance he has in the high hurdles. The 1956 and 1960 Olympic Champion, Lee Calhoun, stood 6-1. Willie May, the 1960 runner-up, was 6-3½. Six feet to six feet three or so seems to be the ideal size for a high hurdler. There have been some great high hurdlers who were not six-footers, but had they been taller they might have been much greater.

High Hurdle Technique

The start of a high hurdle race is just like the start of a dash, except that many boys have to stretch out a bit to get their eight strides to the first hurdle. The action to the first hurdle as well as between hurdles is a sprinting action.

Occasionally, although seldom in high school, there are hurdlers who are very tall and have such a long stride that they must start with the opposite foot ahead and take only seven strides to the first hurdle. But whether the high hurdler takes seven or eight strides to the first hurdle, he should take only three strides between hurdles.

A pronounced lean over the hurdle is a must. A hurdler who does not have that forward lean will ride over the hurdle and will not get back to the ground quickly enough. High hurdling is a diving action. The farther a boy can get his center of gravity forward by getting as much upper body and arm weight out ahead of him, the more quickly he will be able to return to the ground. A hurdler can gain speed only while on the ground, so he must come in contact with the ground as soon as possible after clearing each hurdle. (See Figure 10.)

To help teach our hurdlers to get a good forward lean and to get down fast off the hurdles, we have them all use the double arm thrust in practice. However, in competition, if they have mastered the forward lean, they may use the single arm thrust if they prefer it.

Arm action is an extremely important factor in maintaining balance over the hurdles. The lead arm should be out directly in front of its shoulder and never out to the side or across the hurdler's body. Then when the lead arm is pulled back, the elbow should lead its backward movement.

When the boy approaches each hurdle, his eyes should be focused on the top of the hurdle bar. As soon as he is above the hurdle, he can transfer his gaze to the top of the next hurdle as most hurdlers do, or, if he prefers, look straight down until he is over the barrier.

It is beneficial to the hurdler to straighten his lead leg when clearing the hurdle, but it should be straightened for only an instant. The lead leg should be brought up as in a normal running stride—the knee comes up, the lower leg swings forward and upward, clearing the hurdle bar, and the leg is immediately bent back toward the ground. The hurdler lands on the ball of his lead foot with his center of gravity a little ahead of that foot. He is then ready for his next stride.

The trail leg clears the hurdle in one continuous motion. It is never started forward, delayed, and then jerked through. The trail leg should come through at about the same speed as it would if the boy were striding along on the ground, with no attempt made to hurry the movement or slow it down. The under-side of the trail leg—thigh, calf, ankle bone, and foot—should all barely clear the hurdle.

FIG. 10

High Hurdle Form. Glenn Davis of Ohio
State University, great all-around hurdler
and winner of three Olympic gold medals,
leans far forward as he clears a high hurdle.
(Courtesy *Athletic Journal*)

After the lead foot lands, a long-reaching stride must be taken with the trail leg. Raising the trailing knee higher after coming off the hurdle will help overcome the tendency to chop that all-important step.

Physical Qualifications for the Low Hurdles

Speed is an absolute essential in running the low hurdles just as it is in the highs, but besides speed, a boy who runs the low hurdles must have the strength and physical condition of a quarter-miler. Running a full flight of lows requires greater strength and physical condition than is needed to run either the high hurdles or the 220. If a boy is not able to run a good strong 300, then he probably is not physically ready for a fast flight of either the 180- or 220-yard lows.

Although speed is so necessary in running the low hurdles, we rarely double our sprinters in the lows. We did with Jesse Owens, of course, and he became good enough to break the world record, but he was an exceptional athlete. Sprinters are usually busy enough with the 100 and 220.

Looseness in the hips is not as necessary in the low hurdles as it is in the highs. The runner's crotch is higher than the top bar of the hurdle and when he clears it by an inch or two with his trailing knee, his thigh is extended downward from hip to knee, at an angle of as much as 45 degrees. (See Figure 11.) The trail leg should not be parallel with the top of the hurdle bar the way a high hurdler's must be.

Ten strides to the first hurdle and seven strides between is the way most champions run the low hurdles. The extra-

FIG.11   **Low Hurdle Form.** Jesse Owens of Ohio State University, world record-holder in the 220-yard low hurdles and winner of four Olympic gold medals, runs over a low hurdle. Notice that Owens' hips are well above the hurdle bar. Hip flexibility is not nearly as necessary in running the low hurdles as it is in the highs. (Photo: Ohio State University)

big boy can change his feet at the start and cut one stride
off his approach to the first hurdle.

Alternating the lead leg over the hurdles is sometimes
done. However, as the boy gains strength, he should make
a great effort to run seven strides instead of eight. A boy
who alternates might score points in high school meets but
he will seldom if ever score in college. If the boy has
enough ability for his coach to think he could run the lows,
then he could probably become a pretty good sprinter or
broad jumper as well.

Low Hurdle Technique

Good low-hurdling form comes when the boy is able to
run right over the top of the hurdle without losing his
balance or stride. There is no advantage in having a lot of
body bend. The low hurdler should just maintain his normal running body-lean over the hurdle.

Arm action is extremely important in low hurdling to
help the runner maintain his balance over the hurdles.
The hurdler must stay in balance to keep his rhythm
throughout the race.

The action to the first hurdle and between hurdles is a
sprinting action, just as it is in the highs.

The 400-Meter Hurdles

The question is often raised, "Does the hurdler or does
the quarter-miler make the best performer in the 400-meter
hurdles?" I would say, most of the time it is the hurdler.
A boy must have good hurdle technique to do well in this
event.

Glenn Davis, world record holder and two-time Olympic Champion in the 400-meter hurdles, was a hurdler long before he began running the quarter. He ran the lows in high school and began running the highs and the 440 at Ohio State, where he turned in times of 14 flat and a world record of 45.7 respectively.

Another question often asked is whether the 400-meter hurdles should be added to our high school meets to instill interest in the event. I think that would be a mistake. It would be an Indian file race with 20 or 30 yards between the boys as they finished. There just wouldn't be any competition. Besides, we don't seem to need an interest-builder in this event. The U.S.A. ran first, second, and third in the 400-meter hurdles in both the 1956 and the 1960 Olympic Games.

The usual number of strides taken to the first hurdle in this event is 21, and I would never recommend anything except 15 between hurdles. Charlie Moore won the 1952 Olympic title at Helsinki running 13 strides between hurdles. A week later he ran an exhibition race in London, and because of the muddy track that day, was forced to run 15 strides. He ran faster in the mud using 15 strides than he had run the week before in the Olympics.

There was a time when Davis would take 13 for the first two or three hurdles and then go to 15, but we worked continually to make it a straight 15 throughout the race. It is more like a quarter-mile stride when there are fifteen.

The 400-meter hurdler must have good knowledge of pace. Davis ran notoriously slow for the first 100 yards. If there were runners to the inside of him they would pick up all the stagger before they had run 40 yards. He liked to stride along and stay loose until the last 150 yards or so and then finish hard. I would not recommend that as the best way to run this race, but that is the way he preferred to run and he had great success with it.

Training for the 400-meter hurdles is the same as training for the quarter mile, except that the boy has to practice running over the hurdles. We found that trying to run Davis through a full flight of intermediate hurdles by himself was not a good workout. Unless he was in a race and had someone to run against to give him that extra stimulus, he would go through a flight in 56 to 58 seconds and be through for the day. We found that by having him run five hurdles five times at 400-meter hurdle pace, he would put much more into his workout, and as a result gained both endurance and speed.

Conditioning

I feel that whatever schedule a boy follows to get in condition to run the hurdles is all right, as long as he does what he does to the best of his ability. There are many different ways to get in condition for any event.

This is a sample pre-season workout schedule:

MONDAY: 1. Run an easy 220 (35 seconds). Walk 50 yards. Run another very easy 220.

2. Do loosening calisthenics, but not body-building exercises. (The hurdler must be loose enough in the crotch so he can easily sit in the hurdling position on the ground with his lower leg at a 90-degree angle with his thigh.) Do forward and sideward kicks, alternating legs. Lift one knee and then the other, pulling them up against your chest. Touch your toes with knees stiff. Rotate hips with feet

planted. Lie on the ground and touch your toes to the ground back over your head. Spread your legs 5 to 10 times. (The hurdler must be loose and it will take more than just a few days to achieve this looseness.) Do your stretching exercises at home, too.

3. Run two more 220's (35 seconds).

TUESDAY:
1. Run an easy 220. Walk 50 yards. Run another easy 220.
2. Stretching exercises.
3. If your legs are not too sore, run two more easy 220's.

WEDNESDAY:
1. Stride and jog an easy 440.
2. Stretching exercises.
3. Step over three low hurdles two or three times, taking two extra steps between hurdles. Stride a 220. Walk 100 yards. Stride another 220.

THURSDAY:
1. Run an easy 440 with a little faster stride for the last 50 yards. No sprinting!
2. In addition to your regular stretching exercises, begin doing leg stretches using a high hurdle.
3. Run over three high hurdles five or six times. Begin by taking five strides between them—for form. Stride two 220's (30-32 seconds each).

FRIDAY:
1. Stride a 440 (about 63 seconds).
2. Stretching exercises.
3. Run over three high hurdles five or six times. Stride two 220's.

SATURDAY:
Same workout as Friday. (If your legs are sore, rest Saturday and Sunday.)

When the hurdler's legs begin feeling strong, the coach should have him increase the tempo of his workouts in the

Number 3 section. Sections one and two should be kept the same and, of course, must never be skipped in practice. At the end of the warmup period each day, hurdlers should also begin doing some full-speed running on the flat and over three hurdles.

Two weeks before competition the hurdler should be running over six hurdles. He will gain more by running many repeats over six hurdles than by trying to go through a full flight.

Hurdlers should do their running with the quarter-milers or sprinters, concentrating on repeat work and speed work. For example, our hurdlers may run two sets of fast 150's. (A set can be three, four, five, or six repeats of a given distance.) Six or eight boys get together and with a running start go barreling down the track. They walk back, talking things over and then go through another one. After a 15-minute rest, they are ready for another set. Repeat 150's build both endurance and speed.

The runner should not worry about getting too tired during a workout. When he learns to force himself to go fast and strong all through the workout, that is when real condition arrives. Of course, if he reports for a workout feeling tired, his schedule should be eased a bit.

Before the Meet

On the day of an afternoon meet, eat at 9:30 and then again after the meet, but nothing in between. For a night meet, eat a late breakfast and then a meal in the middle of the afternoon.

We always try to have our hurdlers dressed and on the field an hour before competition so they can warm up slowly and completely and be mentally ready. Every boy should finish his warmup by sprinting a couple of straightaways as hard as he can. Hurdlers must loosen their muscles thoroughly before the race.

Some boys like to have a light rubdown before competition. If possible, give them one. Every trackman who is running more than one race should have a rubdown between races. A boy's legs will feel tired because of the waste products that haven't had a chance to be eliminated. A trainer who knows how to rub will rub toward the heart to help get those waste products out of the muscle tissue.

We talk over the opponents with our hurdlers before a race, unless we know that the opponents are much better than our boys; then we do not mention them.

I think that giving advice to a boy before a race will backfire on the coach as often as it will aid him. If the coach is going to talk with his hurdler before the race, he should tell him to run his own race and stay in his own lane. He should keep his eyes on the top bar of each hurdle and not let his attention waver. If the hurdler watches the other hurdlers in a race, even peripherally, he will probably get himself in trouble.

The best advice I can think of to give a hurdler is: *Get out ahead and improve your position!*

CHAPTER SIX

The Relay Races

CLYDE LITTLEFIELD
University of Texas

CLYDE LITTLEFIELD has developed many track "greats" at the University of Texas since becoming head coach in 1920, but he is probably best known for his record-breaking relay teams. His teams have dominated many of the nationally-known relay meets over the years and have held numerous world records.

At Texas, Littlefield was a 12-letter man, an all-time mark. He was an all-conference football player for two years, all-American basketball player one year, and in track competed in the hurdles and dashes, losing only one race in his entire collegiate career.

A Hall of Fame coach, Littlefield is past-president of the National Collegiate Track Coaches Association and a member of the Olympic and Pan-American Games Committees. In 1952 he was one of the four coaches of the U. S. Olympic Track and Field Team in Helsinki. The following year, he received the Coach of the Year award, the second track coach in the country to ever receive the trophy.

Littlefield's Longhorn track teams have compiled an enviable record over the years, winning 25 Southwest Conference Championships and finishing in the runner-up spot 13 times. Only twice have his teams finished lower than second place.

The Relay Races

Over the years, competing in relay races has become a tradition at the University of Texas. Texas relay teams have held world records in the 440-yard, 880-yard, sprint medley, distance medley, and shuttle relays.

During some seasons, when it seemed we wouldn't be able to come up with enough good boys for a relay team, we have found a hurdler or broad jumper or maybe even a pole vaulter who could run a leg. Somehow, we have always managed to field representative relay teams.

The 440-Yard Relay (4 x 110)

Many sprint relays are won because of good baton exchanges. In many races we have defeated relay teams that had four runners who were faster than our four boys, but whose baton exchanges were not as good.

Our teams use what is called the upward movement in the 440-yard relay exchange. (See Figure 12.) The baton is carried in the left hand and is passed upward into the right hand of the man who is receiving it. The outgoing runner's right elbow is bent and the palm of his hand is down in a position as though he is picking up something off the ground. Except for the anchor man, every member of the team who receives the baton immediately switches it from his right hand to his left.

Another popular baton-passing style is the "inside pass," where the baton is given with the right hand and received

FIG. 12

Sprint Relay Exchange. Hollis Gainey and
Bobby Whilden, members of world-record-
breaking sprint relay teams at Texas, complete another successful baton pass. (Courtesy *Scholastic Coach*)

with the left. This style seems helpful in sprint relays when the exchange must be made on a turn, for it permits the sprinter to lean in more easily as he runs the turn.

The exchange used in the 440-yard relay is a "blind" pass. When the incoming runner reaches a predetermined mark—usually six to nine yards in front of the zone—the outgoing runner begins his run and never looks back.

The two individuals who will be involved in each of the relay's baton exchanges must work out the position of the mark that they will use in their exchange. The position of the mark depends largely upon the starting speed of the man who is to receive the baton.

Every exchange should be made when both men are running at top speed. If the incoming runner overruns the man receiving the baton, then the outgoing runner has not reached top speed at the time of the exchange, and the mark must be moved back a little from the zone line. If the outgoing runner gets away from his teammate before the exchange can be made, the mark should be moved closer to the zone.

To improve our baton passes, the boys run through the exchanges at ½ and ¾ speed. This gives them the feel of the baton and teaches them to better coordinate their movements.

Placing of the runners in the 440-yard relay is very important. Our best man usually runs in the second position. We have often been criticized for this, but I believe that if we can get ahead of the other teams at the first exchange because of a good baton pass and have a good man running, the anchor man does not have to be the fastest man.

Another factor also must be considered when running

the 440-yard relay. In a relay where some of the runners will have to run curves and some will not, the boys must be placed accordingly. Some boys can run curves better than others. I have had some runners who could run better on curves than on a straight-away. Therefore, these boys were placed in a position in the relay where they ran a turn.

The 880-Yard Relay (4 x 220)

The 880 relay is run exactly as the 440 except that the man who is to receive the baton watches the speed of the incoming runner. After the receiver begins driving out, he looks back under his arm. If he sees that the boy coming in isn't going to be able to catch him, he slows down a bit. It is always the responsibility of the outgoing runner, the receiver, to make the exchange right.

A "go" mark is made on the track, as in the 440 relay, but it is not as far out because of the slightly slower rate of speed of the incoming runners in the 880 relay. If the incoming runner's rate of speed appears to be fast, the receiving runner takes off when the mark is hit. But if the incoming runner seems to be tying up, the receiver must wait and judge when to start so that he will not pull away from his teammate before the exchange has been made.

The outgoing runner must receive the baton in one continuous movement without any pause from the moment he drives out until he is in possession of the baton, thus enabling him to get a flying start. The exchange should be made when both men are as near as possible to full speed.

The Mile Relay (4 x 440)

Although baton exchanges are not as important in the mile relay as in the sprint relays, mile relay races are sometimes won because of good exchanges, too.

We use what we call the downward movement in the mile relay exchange. (See Figure 13.) The incoming runner carries the baton in his left hand and hands off with a downward motion. The receiver takes it palm up in his right hand, and he immediately switches it to his left hand.

It is not a blind pass. The outgoing runner watches the man coming in during the exchange. He must judge the speed of the incoming runner and begin his run accordingly.

Usually our second-fastest man runs first in the mile relay and then a man in either the second or third position, who can run better in a relay than in an open quarter. Our slowest man usually runs third but not always. On the team that set the national record in 1959, our slowest man ran second.

If it is likely that we will be behind after two men, we need a good third man who can bring the baton up front to give it to the anchor man. Of course, if your men can keep up with the other teams, always put the fastest man in the anchor position.

The Two-Mile Relay (4 x 880)

The type of baton exchange used in the two-mile relay is the same as that used in the mile relay. But the two-mile relay exchange is not as important as in the shorter race

FIG. 13   **Mile Relay Exchange.** Jimmy Holt passes the baton to anchor man Eddie Southern and the Longhorns are on their way to another mile relay win. Southern's blistering 45.3 anchor leg helped the Texans set a new Texas Relays record of 3:10.4. (United Press Photo)

because the runners are moving slower and therefore are less liable to bungle the exchange. Furthermore, there is more time to make up for errors in the longer race.

The Sprint Medley Relay (440-220-220-880)

In the sprint medley relay, the exchanges are different from those in any other relay. The exchange between the quarter-miler and the first 220 man should be made in the first 10 yards of the exchange zone. This means the quarter-miler will not be running a full 440 and the 220 man will be running more than 220 yards, and, therefore, a little more of the race can be run at the 220 pace than would be if the exchange were made in the center of the zone.

The exchange between the 220 men is exactly the same as in the 880 relay. It is a visual pass using the upward movement.

When the second 220 man hands off to the half-miler, the exchange is made right at the end of the 20-yard zone so that the third man is sprinting almost 230 yards and the half-miler will be running only 870.

Each 220 man is sprinting farther than 220 yards while the quarter-miler and the half-miler are running almost ten yards less than a 440 and 880. This system of passing, if followed properly, will gain precious yardage for the sprint medley relay team.

Training

Our boys get in condition to run the relays by training for their individual events. If they are sprinters, they train as sprinters; if they are quarter-milers, they train as quarter-milers. The only extra workout is in learning to exchange the baton.

In the fall, we work continually on timing. During the season we work on baton passes twice a week, never taking more than six exchanges at a time. Most of our learning is done at ½ and ¾ speed just to improve coordination in handling the baton. Because of the danger of muscle pulls, only once in a while will the boys get in their zones and run the exchanges at full speed.

The main part of each boy's workout is in training for his individual event. He must condition his body to run his own event well before he can become a good relay team member.

The boys must be taught to believe in themselves and have confidence—but never overconfidence. Confidence in his own ability comes to an individual through his training. Because he has confidence in himself, a boy who is ready to run never worries about a race. He knows what he can do because he is in condition to run.

CHAPTER SEVEN

The Pole Vault

Ralph M. Higgins
Oklahoma State University

RALPH M. HIGGINS was named track and cross-country coach at Oklahoma State in 1935. Since then his teams have won many championships, including 17 consecutive Missouri Valley Conference track titles when the school was in that league. His 1954 cross-country team won the NCAA title.

Although he has coached many great performers in every event of track and field, Higgins has become best known in recent years for his outstanding pole vaulters. Three of his Oklahoma State vaulters have been over the fifteen-foot barrier consistently.

During his competitive days at OSU, Higgins was a three-sports man. He played halfback in football, guard in basketball, and was Southwest Conference 100-yard and 440-yard champion.

Between 1950 and 1960, Higgins coached a number of U. S. all-star track and field teams in international competition. He took American athletes on four foreign tours and to the 1960 Rome Olympics, where he was one of the four U. S. coaches.

Higgins served for eight straight years on the NCAA Track and Field Rules Committee and was on both the 1956 and 1960 Olympic Committees.

The Pole Vault

In 1950, the National AAU pole vault record was 14 feet. In the 1960 AAU meet, just ten years later, 16 boys cleared 14-4; 11 of those went over 14-8, and six made 15-0¾, the winning height.* The Olympic record was upped from 14-3¼ to 15-5⅛ during those same ten years.

One of the most important factors contributing to the great improvements in vaulting marks during recent years is hard work. The young men of today, having such high goals set up before them, simply work harder than ever before.

Other factors contributing to the recent improvements in pole vaulting marks and to the consistency of modern-day vaulters as well, are better runways, safer pits, and much-improved training programs.

Physical Qualifications

If I were going to select a boy to become a pole vaulter and had my choice of any type of boy, I would pick one who stands at least 6-3. Besides height, he would have to have inherent speed, agility, and would be an accomplished gymnast.

With regard to high school youngsters, I used to consider only their vaulting marks, but now I realize that many factors influence whether a boy is able to become a

---

* EDITOR's NOTE: Aubrey Dooley of Oklahoma State was the winner on the fewer-misses rule.

good college vaulter or not. Most of the great pole vaulters of today are over six feet in height; most are better than average sprinters, and all are both strong and agile. Height and speed, of course, must be inherent in the vaulter, but strength and agility can be developed through weight training and work on the horizontal bar or other gym apparatus.

Vaulting Form

Jim Graham and Aubrey Dooley, both consistent 15-foot vaulters when they were at Oklahoma State, used vaulting styles that were completely different. Graham, like most of the taller vaulters of today, was a conventional pendulum-swing style vaulter, while Dooley used the spring of his pole to help shoot him over the top. The swing vaulter swings up and over. The spring-type uses the bend of his pole to help him.

The swing vaulter. Because there are so many tall pole vaulters nowadays,* the pendulum-swing has become the most common vaulting style. (See Figure 14.) The taller a boy is, the higher the handgrip he will be able to take on the pole, thus increasing the possibility of his vaulting higher. Graham was able to use the swing style very effectively, since his height allowed him a handgrip ** of 13-8, one of the highest grips of all the better modern-day vaulters.

---

* EDITOR's NOTE: Eleven of the 15 pole vaulters in the 1960 Olympic Team Trials were over six feet tall. Jim Graham was the tallest at 6-4½. Aubrey Dooley at 5-11 was one of the shortest. The winner, Don Bragg, who set a new record of 15-9¼, was 6-3.

** The handgrip is measured from the top of the upper (right) hand to the lower end of the pole.

In the swing style, the vaulter's left hand slides up to his right so that his hands are together on the pole at the take-off. He then lets the forward swing of the lower part of his body carry him on up until his feet are higher than his head.

At the end of this swing-up action, he pulls with his arms and drives his right leg as high above the bar as possible. The pull then blends into a pushup, and at the same time, the vaulter's body begins to turn so that he will be facing the bar as he crosses it. The arms are straightened before the pole is released and the bar is cleared with a flyaway action.

The spring vaulter. This vaulting style seems to have definite advantages for pole vaulters of below-average height. The shorter vaulter who is not able to vault effectively at the higher heights because of his inability to get a high enough handgrip may use the spring style to good advantage. Good pole-bending technique can make up for the handicap brought about by a lack of height.

Dooley's ability to utilize an exceptionally deep pole-bend was largely responsible for his success as a vaulter. At the time of the pole plant and take-off, his left hand was not shifted up to the right, as is usually the rule in pole vaulting. Instead, he kept his hands about a foot apart to facilitate the bending of the pole. (See Figure 15.)

Form used by the spring vaulter is practically the same as that of the swing-type, except that the spring vaulter deliberately bends the pole during his swing. Like most other vaulters who depend on pole-bend to snap them upwards, Dooley used a Fiberglas pole because of its unusually fine flexibility. When Dooley was vaulting at his best, it was not unusual for his pole to bend more than

FIG. 14   **The Swing Style.** Jim Graham of Oklahoma State University, NCAA pole vault champion and Olympic team member, uses the conventional pendulum-swing vaulting style. He lets the forward swing of the lower part of his body

carry him up until his feet are higher than his head. Then
he pulls with his arms, drives his right leg high above
the bar, pushes up and turns, and clears the bar using
the arch-flyaway. (*Daily Oklahoman* photos by Bob Albright)

FIG. 15   **The Spring Style.** Aubrey Dooley of Oklahoma State, 1960 National AAU pole vault champion, uses the spring of his pole to shoot him over the top. Notice that his hands are kept about a foot apart to help bring about the extreme bending of the pole. (*Daily Oklahoman* photo by Bob Albright)

three feet out of line during the swing. Then the straightening of the pole would give him added upward lift when it was needed at the peak of the vault.

Timing is especially important to the spring-type vaulter. When using a very flexible pole, the vaulter must delay his pushup and release until the last moment. But at the peak of the vault when the pole is straightening, he must work faster than usual to finish the vault.

Handgrip and Pole Carry. In any vaulting style, the vaulter must establish the height at which he will grip the pole. His handgrip should be as high as he can possibly reach and still be effective in his vaulting. Then, as the bar is raised, vaulting form is changed slightly, but *the height of the handgrip does not change more than six inches.*

There are a number of acceptable pole-carrying positions, although most of today's better vaulters carry it in a straight-ahead position, parallel with the ground. The right hand, palm down, grasps the pole with the fingers on the inside and the thumb on the outside. The left hand, about three feet below the right, grasps the pole with the fingers on top and the thumb underneath. (See Figure 16.)

The run and pole plant. There should be only one checkmark along the runway, and that should be about one-third of the way to the box. A vaulter doesn't have time after running one-third of the distance to try to hit another mark and still be ready to vault. Graham's total run was 117 feet with a mark 74 feet from the box. Dooley ran 115 feet with a mark at 72 feet.

The vaulter continues his drive right on down to the pole plant. I prefer the underhand style of planting the pole while the arms are still down in the pole-carrying

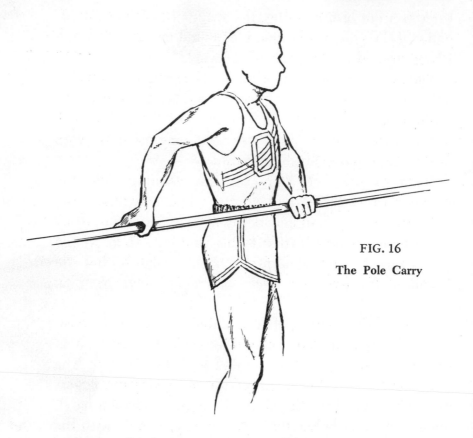

FIG. 16

The Pole Carry

position. This helps to prevent the tendency to raise the pole too early and cause a faulty take-off.

The vault. On the next to last step, the vaulter shifts his left hand up to his right. The right hand remains fixed; it does not move down. As the left hand is shifted, the pole is raised directly above the vaulter's head with the right hand. His arms are flexed to absorb the shock of the take-off. Then his left foot strikes the ground for the take-off in much the same manner as the take-off for the high jump or broad jump and he drives his right knee upward.

The vaulter's head is back and his arms are still flexed

slightly as he swings forward on the pole. Then, when his feet are higher than his head, he doubles his knees and begins to pull with his arms. In that same continuous motion, his right leg is driven high above the crossbar bringing about the turn of the body and getting the vaulter into the push-off position. He then clears the bar using the arch-flyaway, releasing first the left hand—which is lower on the pole—then the right. The arms are lifted above and away from the bar in order to avoid tipping it off.

Finishing the vault. As the vaulter is flying away from his pole, gravity begins to bring his legs down so that he is draped over the crossbar. (See Figure 17.) At this point, getting away from the bar, or "finishing the vault," takes a great deal of skill and coordination.

The vaulter must remember that as the bar gets higher it will take him longer to get above it, so there must be a delay before he begins his swing and his pull and turn.

It is not uncommon to see a vaulter reach out with his feet too early in the vault because he pulled too early and expended his momentum too soon. Or, he may get above the crossbar and knock it off because he was too anxious and tried to get away from it before completing his pushup.

When Dooley began clearing 14 feet and 14-6 regularly, he started shooting for 15 feet, but was not quite able to make it. He was not flying off the pole the same at this new height as he had been at lower heights, so I told him to begin vaulting to see how far he could land in the back of the pit. To land in the back of the pit he would have to fly off the end of his pole and not merely drop straight down.

That day he vaulted ten or more times at 14-6 while

FIG. 17   "Finishing the Vault." This maneuver takes
a great deal of skill and coordination when
the vaulter's body is draped over the crossbar. (Photo: Oklahoma State University)

concentrating on landing as far back in the pit as he could. On the following day he found he was able to fly away from the pole much better than before, so he put the bar up to 15 feet and cleared it on his first attempt.

Bob Richards, the 1952 and 1956 Olympic pole vaulting champion, was able to fly away from his pole better than anyone else I've ever seen. His ability to finish the vault on top more than compensated for his size (5-10) and the height of his pole grip (13-4). When Richards was vaulting at heights above 15 feet, he would get to the top of his vault and keep ascending right off the end of the pole. His handgrip was often more than two feet below the height he was clearing.

Pre-season Conditioning

At the beginning of each school year I give the boys a mimeographed sheet of instructions regarding diet and sleep, but then leave it to them to put these instructions into effect. Young men should be taught to discipline themselves and to develop their own will-power. They can never be very successful without these traits.

Athletes should try to get eight hours of sleep and develop regular eating habits. They should eat at mealtimes and refrain from eating between meals.

We have a weight chart in our locker room on which is kept a daily record of each vaulter's weight. Vaulters soon learn how important it is to avoid excess weight, especially during the season. When Dooley came to OSU as a freshman he weighed 185. As a senior he was vaulting at 160.

In the fall our vaulters work out three days a week. They come out on the track, take three or four laps of easy running, and do 15 to 20 minutes of general stretching exercises. Then after six or seven 75- to 100-yard runs, they are ready to go to work on their vaulting.

When Graham was a senior, he decided he would run on the cross-country team instead of vaulting in the fall. He worked hard all season and even ran in a meet or two.

That winter, Graham was in the gym shooting baskets and was amazed to find that he was able to jump much higher than ever before. We found that since the previous spring his jumping had increased six inches. We believe that cross-country running was largely responsible for increasing the spring in his legs.

During the winter months our vaulters work hard to lay the foundation for what they will do in the spring. We have no indoor vaulting facilities at OSU, so a great deal of our work is done on the horizontal bar and in the weight room.

Weight-lifting is done daily throughout the winter. Our vaulters concentrate on general body-building, with more emphasis on the lighter weights than on heavy lifting.

Workouts

The number of vaults a boy can take in a meet and still be effective depends upon his physical condition. Pole vaulters must be in top physical condition to be able to compete and do well for the length of time it usually takes to run off the vault. They are often the first to get out on the field and the last to leave. To condition our vaulters we have them do a lot of repeat work. They may run six hard 220's in a practice session followed by a number of short dashes.

Our vaulters continue training with light weights throughout the season, but they limit their lifting to the first three days of each week. Occasionally, their workouts consist only of work on the horizontal bar to help develop arms and shoulders.

When vaulting in practice, the bar should be put up to a height where the vaulter will really have to work—even out of reach sometimes. I've seen vaulters who looked great in a meet at 13-6, but lost their form completely at 14 feet, simply because it was a height they had never attempted before. If a vaulter has not had the experience of vaulting at a certain height, a meet is not the place to get that experience.

When a vaulter is improving, we put the bar up to a height he has not yet cleared and tell him to vault at it. When he begins clearing that height with some regularity, the bar is put up even higher.

Each individual vaulter has his own particular faults which have to be corrected in practice. For example, there was a time when Graham was coming down on the crossbar with his chest on every vault. We found that he was unable to see the bar while he was vaulting and so didn't have any idea where it was until he came down on it. To correct this, Graham himself developed an exercise where he did a kind of handspring over a low hurdle, looking at the hurdle as he went over. From this exercise he soon became conscious of where the crossbar was in his vaulting and he became much more consistent.

The injuries that frequently occur in pole vaulting, particularly those involving the ankles, have been reduced in recent years due to the great improvements in runways and landing pits. It is still advisable, however, for every vaulter to have his ankles taped before vaulting.

Before the Meet

The workout on the day before a meet is very light, unless the meet is not very important and the vaulters need to prepare for a later competition. Under those circumstances they would work much harder.

On the night before competition we let the boys use their own judgment as far as sleep is concerned. If a boy is told to go to bed at 9 or 10 o'clock and he isn't used to it, he will toss and roll and won't really get much rest. If the boys want to stay up and watch television and then sleep a little later in the morning, I think that's fine.

On the day of the meet our vaulters don't eat anything after five hours before the time of competition. Their warmup is about the same as before practice. They jog, do their stretching exercises, and take a few "run-throughs." Then they are ready to vault.

CHAPTER EIGHT

The High Jump

ED FLANAGAN
Boston University

ED FLANAGAN, a member of the Boston University coaching staff since 1947, has developed national champions, Olympic champions, and world record holders. Heading the list of great athletes Flanagan has coached is his sensational high jump champion, John Thomas. Thomas successfully recovered from a foot injury at the end of his freshman year at BU to later raise the world standard to 7-3¾.

A former national champion at Holy Cross, Flanagan is considered by many to be the country's foremost expert on the 16-pound hammer and 35-pound weight. He has developed the United States' only 200-foot hammer throwers: Al Hall, Cliff Blair, John Lawlor, and Olympic champion Harold Connolly. Connolly, who holds the world record for the hammer throw, was also the first man to toss the 35-pound weight more than 70 feet. Flanagan is advising former Tufts weightman Bob Backus, who set a world record in the 35-pound event a few weeks prior to Connolly's record heave.

Before joining the BU staff, Flanagan coached at the Los Angeles Athletic Club, Los Angeles Junior College, Andover Academy, and Harvard.

The High Jump

High jumpers are born—not made. A jumper must be gifted with natural spring in his legs and must come to his coach with the innate ability to jump. All a coach can do is to help develop what the boy was born with.

Coaching the high jump differs from coaching other field events. I can show a jumper different styles and let him try them. And I can show him where he is making mistakes. But I could never say to a boy that I'm going to teach him to high jump and he's going to learn to be great.

A great asset to the high jumper is learning to jump at an early age before he is fully grown. The boy can then learn to lay out along the bar and coordinate his body. It is much easier for a boy to learn body coordination when he is young than when he is fully grown.

Coordination is essential to the science of high jumping. The whole science is to get on and off the bar immediately —in a split second—without knocking the bar off. This movement takes coordination. If the boy has begun to develop that coordination at an early age before he has matured, he will be much better able to perfect his high jumping technique later on.

Jumping Styles

The two most common jumping styles used today are the straddle roll and the western roll. In each of these there are two variations—the orthodox jump and the dive.

So there are actually four different styles that are common to modern-day high jumping. These styles are orthodox straddle, dive straddle, orthodox western, and dive western.

The style a beginning jumper should use depends on his physical nature. A new high jump candidate at Boston University spends the first two weeks of practice using his own jumping style without a word from the coaching staff. This gives us a chance to study his style with a view to making any future adaptations that might prove helpful. We adapt the jumping style to the boy—never the boy to a style. A coach who tries to force a jumper to use a particular style that is unsuited for him may hamper the boy's natural ability.

In the orthodox straddle, a jumper who takes off from his left foot will approach the bar from the left. He stops forward progress by planting his left foot at the point of take-off and by leaning back from the bar. He then kicks the right (outside) foot while converting his momentum into a straight-up take-off before rolling over the bar. As his legs are straddling the crossbar at the peak of his jump, his chest is toward the bar and directly above it. The knee of the bent trail leg is still below the bar at this point and the head begins to drop slightly. As the lead leg crosses the bar, the jumper begins to roll. Next, he straightens his trail leg for clearance and drops toward the pit, landing first on his right foot and hand and then on his right side. (See Figure 18.)

The chief difference between the orthodox straddle and the dive straddle is that in using the dive straddle the jumper's head leads the jump and crosses the bar before the lead leg. Thus his head and shoulders precede his hips over and drop down in a kind of dive. This action facilitates clearance of the trail leg, but the style is somewhat complex and therefore demands more precise timing. When employing the dive straddle, the jumper has more of a tendency to lean into the bar during the take-off than when using the orthodox roll.

The whole secret of high jumping is to jump practically straight up so that the center of gravity is then over the take-off foot and to begin the roll only upon reaching maximum height.

The orthodox western roll is much like the orthodox straddle in the take-off: the approach, the gather, and the kick are similar. (See Figure 19.) But in the western roll the jumper lays out over the crossbar on his side and must therefore clear the bar with the entire width of his hips. Because he is wider in this position than when straddling the bar, the jumper must raise his center of gravity higher in order to clear his hips.

However, converting from western to straddle jumping is not always possible. Some jumpers cannot change to the straddle roll and coordinate at the bar. They're just not physically mobile enough and so must stick with the western roll.

In the dive western, as in the dive straddle, the jumper's head leads the rest of his body over the crossbar. The main drawback of the dive western style is the risk of not achieving a vertical take-off. Because of this, there is a tendency for the jumper to lean toward the bar too early in the jump.

FIG. 18   **Orthodox Straddle Form.** John Thomas of Boston University, national high jump champion and world record-holder, clears the bar at 7 feet 1½ inches. Notice Thomas'

backward lean and vicious kick at the take-off and his
roll at the peak of the jump which keeps his trail leg
from knocking the bar off. (Courtesy *Scholastic Coach*)

FIG. 19   **The Western Roll.** Walt Davis of Texas A & M, 1952 Olympic high jump champion, demonstrates the western roll that he used to clear 6 feet 11⅝ inches. Notice the similarity in the take-off of the western roll and the orthodox

straddle. The main difference between the two styles is the position of the jumper above the crossbar. The western roll jumper pulls his trail leg under him, clearing the bar on his side. (Courtesy *Athletic Journal*)

Orthodox Straddle Form

Of all the jumping styles, I believe that the orthodox straddle will be most prevalent in the future of high jumping. John Thomas used it to perfection as he pushed the world record from 7-1 on up to 7-3¾ in one season. It took 20 years and four record holders to produce the previous 2¾-inch increase.*

All of our straddle jumpers use a seven-stride approach which is now becoming almost standard. We approach the crossbar with just a fair amount of speed, to give the body momentum, and then stop forward progress at the point of the take-off by planting the take-off foot and leaning back from the bar.

The seven-stride approach is very rhythmic. The first four strides give the jumper the momentum he needs in his approach to the bar. The final three strides are much more rapid than the first four, and during these comes the gather for the jump.

The jumper's legs are slightly flexed as he drops lower in a gather on the last three steps. With the final stride, the jumper is leaning back away from the bar to get additional upward drive from the next-to-last step as well as from the take-off. Most jumpers fail to lean back during their last step. The tendency is to move too far forward rather than get their center of gravity directly over the take-off foot.

We jump at a point one foot to the right of the center of the crossbar and take off one and one-half feet from its plane. The angle of approach is 37 degrees. At that par-

---

* *Track and Field News*, July 1960, p. 4.

ticular angle we have found that the jumper can most successfully get on and off the bar.

When taking off, a high jumper hits with the back of his heel first, and then rocks up on his toe as he is leaving the ground. To assure him of firm footing, we have heel spikes placed in each shoe as far back as they can be put.

To develop kicking action, we have the jumper kick at what we call 6 o'clock. His take-off leg represents the hour hand of a clock and his lead leg is the minute hand. He approaches the bar, plants his take-off foot, and drives his lead leg up past 6:15 straight up toward 6 o'clock before his rear toe leaves the ground.

The momentum of a kick near 6 o'clock will carry the jumper straight up, while with a 6:15 kick, he will tend to ride along the bar because of centrifugal force. John Thomas is the only jumper I've ever seen who could kick almost straight up. Some of his greatest jumps have been near 6 o'clock.

At the point of take-off, there is a natural tendency to kick into the crossbar instead of beside it. We try to overcome this by keeping the jumper's right arm passive and his left arm active. If a hurdler who leads with his right leg were to thrust his right arm forward at the same time, he would turn to the side. In high jumping the same is true. To keep from kicking into the bar, the jumper should thrust his left arm forward as he leaves the ground. He should kick viciously with his right leg and lead with the opposite arm.

If the kick is vicious enough, the roll will come naturally. The kick is the action; the reaction starts the turn without any deliberate effort. The trick is to stop the jumper from rolling so that part of his body is not coming down while he is actually on his way up.

At the peak of the jump, the boy's trunk and lead leg are just above the bar and almost parallel to it. He then leads his fall into the pit with his right arm and leg.

Common Jumping Errors

The most common mistake by straddle jumpers is in straightening or "kicking" the trail leg while laying out over the crossbar. There should never be a kick after the jumper has left the ground. It accomplishes nothing.

Another fault is in rolling too much at the bar. Instead of jumping first for height and then rolling, some jumpers start putting a leg over and begin rolling from the moment they leave the ground. When this is done, the jumper is not getting as much height as he would if he were concentrating more on the jump and less on the roll.

On the other hand, some jumpers do not roll enough at the bar. They are face down over the bar and are still face down when they land in the pit. The proper landing for a right-footed straddle jumper is on his right hand and side. This is one fault that can be corrected easily, however. A more vicious kick will cause the roll to come naturally.

Some boys fall apart at a height they've never jumped before. Sometimes they never get off the ground when the bar is only one inch higher than the mark they just cleared. One inch should never completely dissolve a man's jumping form. When a boy approaches the bar at a height he has never achieved, encourage him to make the same effort that he made at the previous height. There's no excuse for falling apart.

Occasionally, a jumper will imitate another's style in trying to improve himself. I know of two jumpers in the East who have tried to copy John Thomas' form, and both have hurt themselves as high jumpers. Because Thomas holds the world record, they feel that his is the correct way to jump, so they are attempting to learn to jump with a straight lead leg as he does. Of course, it was the best way for John to jump, but his way might not be the best style for someone of a completely different physical make-up. A jumper should stick to the style that he has found to be most effective for him.

Fall Workouts

FIRST WEEK—Begin with easy jogging plus 20 minutes of stretching exercises. Then jog a mile, walk five minutes, jog a mile, walk five minutes, jog a mile.

At Boston University, one-half hour every day is spent learning the fundamentals of a new event called a "hobby event." Each boy chooses the event that he would like to learn to master. For example, John Thomas' hobby event was throwing the javelin from a standing position. During his freshman year, he threw 156 feet. The following fall when he came back to school, we taught him the last five steps in the approach for throwing the javelin, and with that short run he threw 190 feet. That's when it ceased to be just a hobby event.

SECOND WEEK—Any new high jump candidate is asked to jump during this week using his own jumping style with no coaching suggestions. On the last day of the week he jumps as high as he can. It is then decided what jumping style should be adapted to the boy's physical abilities.

On Tuesdays and Thursdays, veteran high jumpers jump at the height at which their weaknesses begin to show.

Six Weeks Prior to Meets

We call Monday "kickday." Each jumper spends 15 minutes every Monday approaching the bar and kicking his lead leg up without actually jumping.

Monday is also the day our jumpers do most of their running. Although the workout usually consists of just two 220's, on the Monday preceding his first seven-foot jump of the 1960 season, John Thomas ran six 220's in 26 seconds each, walking one lap between them.

On Tuesdays we jump for endurance. If a boy has a little flaw in his jumping form, we try to help him correct it— *at a height where the flaw will show up!* Many jumpers try to correct their form at a height that they can easily clear, but that's not the same as jumping higher. The tendency to "lose form" while attempting a peak performance is more common in the high jump and pole vault than in any of the other events.

On Wednesdays, we jump for height, but we jump under meet conditions. We begin jumping at the height that the meet will probably start and at the interval of time we think we will be forced to take because of the number of entries. After clearing the bar at each height, the boys must wait several minutes before jumping again. During a Wednesday workout, a boy may take only seven jumps during the hour's workout.

We do a little running and weight work on Thursdays. On Friday we rest.

SAMPLE SCHEDULE

MONDAY: 15 minutes of vigorous stretching exercises.
15 minutes perfecting the timing of strides in approaching the bar, kicking the lead leg as high as it will go without actually jumping.
Two 220's in 26 seconds with a five-minute interval.
Easy jogging to finish the hour's work.

TUESDAY: Endurance Day.
10 minutes of stretching exercises plus five minutes of easy jogging.
Intensive jumping for 45 minutes with no rest, at the height where weaknesses begin to show.

WEDNESDAY: 10 minutes of stretching and five minutes of jogging.
Jump for height under meet conditions, taking the same amount of time between jumps that might be taken in competition.

THURSDAY: 15 minutes of very light weight-lifting and five minutes of easy jogging.

FRIDAY: No practice.

During the Season

After competition begins, the workout schedule is the same as for preseason with these exceptions:

1. If the meet is on a Friday rather than Saturday, Monday's workout is eliminated.

2. After the first one-third of the season, if traveling to and from a meet is long and tiring, the workout on the following Monday is eliminated.

3. If in the last third of the season an athlete is razor sharp and consistent, his Monday workouts are eliminated.

Body Building

We want the high jumper to develop the muscles that are going to be needed for his jumping, of course, but we want him to develop the rest of his body, too, so that no one part of his body will act as a detriment to his jumping. We are not interested in developing weight-lifters.

A novice is always accompanied to the weight room by the coach or an experienced lifter and is taught the correct lifting procedures. We always begin with weights that can be handled easily. When the beginner shows an understanding of the lifts, he moves into a gradually stepped-up program.

Since high jumpers vary in size and strength, it is impossible to say what the starting poundage should be in any lift. The poundage will vary with the individual, of course. Starting with a weight he can easily handle, the jumper should gradually progress to weights that will offer him more resistance.

Our jumpers concentrate on using the Leg Press Machine, the prone press, the military press, and weighted shoes.

The best form of weight training for the high jump is the Leg Press Machine. The jumper lies on his back and presses the weight upward with his legs completely doubled and slowly lifts the weight until his legs are straight. Thomas lifted up to 490 pounds on the Leg Press Machine to develop his heavy thigh and calf muscles. For endurance he did 10 lifts in succession. Then he would drop to 75 pounds, pressing that with his legs, and flicking it up with his toes at the peak of his lift. This developed the muscles for his take-off.

Sample Body Building Schedule

This schedule is one used by John Thomas and is probably far beyond the average jumper's capabilities. A common sense viewpoint will adust the specific amount of weight that should be lifted in each case.

A. Leg Press Machine
    1. Ten lifts of 280 pounds
    2. Ten lifts of 330 pounds
    3. Ten lifts of 390 pounds

B. Prone Press
    1. Ten lifts of 160 pounds
    2. Ten lifts of 180 pounds
    3. Ten lifts of 190 pounds

C. Military Press
    1. Ten lifts of 140 pounds
    2. Ten lifts of 160 pounds
    3. Ten lifts of 180 pounds

D. High Kicks (executed while grasping a fence or rail with inside arm)
    1. Ten kicks with three-pound shoe
    2. Ten kicks with five-pound shoe
    3. Ten kicks with seven-pound shoe
    4. In the future we plan to use a 10-pound shoe, too.

Prior to the Meet

Our jumpers eat three hours before the competition begins and try to start warming up about an hour before.

They check their steps, take 10 to 12 minutes of the same stretching exercises that are used in practice, and then do some fairly hard running. During the final half hour before the high jump competition begins, they bend and stretch for 15 minutes and relax the final 15 before jumping.

CHAPTER NINE

The Broad Jump

GORDON FISHER
Indiana University

GORDON FISHER has been a prominent figure on the American college coaching scene for many years. Before joining the Indiana University staff in 1944, Fisher was head football and track coach at North Central College where he enjoyed unusual success for 18 years. At Indiana Fisher's teams have won three Big Ten championships and have consistently ranked in the upper level.

Fisher began his outstanding career in track and field while attending high school at Cavalier, North Dakota. He scored 13 points as a member of the 1914 state championship track team and was the individual high scorer in the 1915 state meet. That year he won the shot-put with one of the first state records of over 50 feet, the broad jump, the discus throw, the javelin throw, was second in the hammer throw, and ran the anchor leg on the second place relay team.

Under Fisher, Indiana trackmen have set two world records and have bettered 13 of 18 all-time Indiana records. In the 1956 Olympics, he was the only U. S. coach to provide two gold medal winners, broad jumper Greg Bell and Decathlon Champion Milt Campbell.

The Broad Jump

According to Mortensen and Cooper,* Greg Bell of Indiana, the Olympic broad-jump winner of 1956, combined what many coaches believe are the ideal essentials in correct broad jumping. He had a relaxed run to the take-off, good lead-leg swing, arched back with chest and head up to assure proper hip swing, and good landing position.

The three qualities most essential to broad jumping are great speed to the take-off to give the athlete momentum for the jump, good height to avoid as long as possible the return to earth, and fully extended legs to get the greatest possible distance out of the jump.

The jumper must not only have speed, but he must be able to utilize that speed at the right time. He must have the ability to get to the take-off board in such a manner that he has great speed at the time he leaves the board.

The jumper must be able to get height and, of course, he cannot get good height without springy leg muscles. Bell and one of his teammates at Indiana could go over a high jump crossbar in a broad jump position and clear very close to six feet.

The jumper also has to have good body control. Certain positions must be assumed in the air which require good control of his muscular set-up.

A long-legged jumper has an advantage over a boy who is not very tall. It is natural for a boy with long legs to

---

* Jesse P. Mortensen and John M. Cooper, *Track and Field for Coach and Athlete* (Englewood Cliffs, N.J.: Prentice-Hall, Inc., 1959), p. 136.

assume a higher position in the air and to reach a little farther with his legs when landing in the pit. Ralph Boston and Bo Roberson, first- and second-place finishers in the 1960 Olympic broad jump, stood 6-1½ and 6-1, respectively. On the other hand, Greg Bell, who won the Olympic title four years before, stood only 5-8½ and was rather short-legged. But Bell was able to make up for his short legs with the tremendous leg extension he was able to get before landing in the pit. I don't know of another jumper who could or can extend his legs in the air the way Bell did.

Selecting Broad Jumpers

Because the requirements for the broad jump are similar to those for several other events, we find that many athletes who participate in other events also broad jump. Those in the sprints, for example, may be encouraged to try the broad jump because of the speed required for both events. Likewise, the similarity between low hurdling and broad jumping makes the low hurdler a potential candidate for the broad jump, too. The low hurdler must have the same speed, agility, and evenness of stride that is required for the broad jump.

Since the approach on the runway in pole vaulting is so similar to the broad jump approach, pole vaulters often can make the change to the broad jump, too. Bell was a pole vaulter in high school until his senior year when an injury forced him to drop out of that event and take up broad jumping.

The Run

The length of run for the broad jump should vary according to the maturity of the individual. A more mature athlete can profit by taking a longer run than a high school boy can use. The ordinary high school jumper should run about 100 feet, the college boy 120 to 125 feet, and the mature athlete 140 feet or more.

In order to maintain top speed to the take-off, I recommend that only one checkmark be used, and that mark should be near the beginning of the run. The final portion of the run is where the jumper must have unhesitating speed. A jumper cannot concentrate on checkmarks and run at top speed at the same time.

Bell ran a total distance of 140 to 142 feet, taking four leisurely strides to his checkmark at approximately 120 feet and then running at full speed from there to the board. As wind and track conditions would vary on certain days, the mark would be altered somewhat. He ran at full effort until he was 50 or 60 feet from the board, where he would concentrate on relaxation, continuing his speed without continued maximum effort.

The Take-Off

When Bell approached the board, he would keep his eyes on it until he was two or three strides away and then look up. He seldom fouled, but whenever he did have a bad day with the board, he would keep his vision on the board a little longer. Until a jumper is really experienced, I tell him to keep his eyes on the board until he hits it.

There is a settling of the body in the last couple of strides before the jump. It seems to come about naturally, without any particular thought. Then when the jumper hits the board, he drives for height.

Form in the Air

There are two main broad jumping styles. One is the straight-away jump or the knee-tuck style as it is often called. In this style both legs immediately assume a forward position in the air. The other is the hitch kick or alternating leg action style, known to many coaches and athletes as "running in air." (See Figure 20.)

The straight-away jump is easier to learn than the hitch kick because of its simplicity, but there is one big drawback to this style of broad jumping. Because the legs are immediately brought to a forward position, a jumper using a straight-away jump cannot keep his legs fully extended throughout the jump. The pull of gravity through the entire distance in the air causes the legs to drop more quickly than if the legs are brought to the forward position after ⅔ of the jump is completed, as in the hitch kick style. By having the legs assume the extended position just before landing, the hitch kick jumper has delayed the pull of gravity.

Bell used the hitch kick with great effectiveness. Even though he was short-legged, he was able to reach out with his legs on landing and get extra distance because of the delay of gravity and his excellent leg extension.

He would take off from his left foot and his right leg would go forward. Then his legs reversed positions—the right leg back and the left forward to remain there. Finally, the right leg would come forward beside the left so that both were in an extended position for the landing.

As Bell hit the board, he would begin his drive for height with an upward thrust of his arms until both arms were well above his head at the peak of the jump. When we discussed this movement, he said that he was not conscious of it at all, so we never made any effort to add to that arm action or change it. It was one of the natural movements of one jumper that might not be natural for another.

Other great jumpers have used the hitch kick style, too. Jesse Owens, who held the world broad jump record for more than 25 years, used it, as did Ralph Boston, who broke Owens' record.

Landing

It is a serious mistake, of course, for a jumper to fall back or sit down in the pit as he lands, since this is the point from which his jump will be measured. It is just as serious a mistake for him to go forward on his hands after he has made his jump. Falling forward is proof that the jumper's feet were not extended far enough in front of him before landing in the pit.

To get the most possible distance the jumper must reach with his legs for every inch he can get, but he must not reach so far that he cannot control the final phase of his landing. His entire body should be behind his feet upon contact with the sand. Then as he lands, his knees and hips fold forward so he doesn't sit back into the pit.

FIG. 20

The Hitch-Kick. Greg Bell of Indiana University, 1956 Olympic broad jump champion, uses the hitch-kick style to set a new NCAA record of 26 feet 7 inches. Notice his drive for height from the board and the forward position of his arms and legs before landing. (Courtesy *Athletic Journal*)

Common Injuries

The most common broad jumping injury is the heel bruise. To try to prevent these bruises, we used to have our jumpers put sponge rubber pads in the heels of their shoes, but we never found them to be very effective. In recent years, a heel cup has been devised that not only protects the heel and prevents bruises but also will allow an athlete to keep going by slipping one of these cups in his shoe even after a heel has been bruised.

The broad jumper, like most athletes, is subject to muscle pulls. Although warming up properly and exercising thoroughly are possible preventatives, many jumpers who warm up and exercise properly still suffer pulled muscles. It appears that some athletes are more liable to muscle pulls. In such cases special precautions, such as protective taping, should be taken.

Fall Track

The number of days our broad jumpers spend working out each week during the fall depends upon their academic schedule. We like to have them out three days a week if possible. The workouts consist of warming up, calisthenics, and short repeat runs. Repeats of 200 yards are the longest. The boys run a lot of 80's and 110's.

At Indiana not much work has been done with specialized muscle development exercises as yet, but this type of training is definitely coming. Coaches and athletes have had their eyes opened in recent years by the great improvements in track and field which have been attributed chiefly to the use of resistance exercises. The results have been so outstanding that we cannot help recognizing the value of these exercises. (See Appendix.)

During the Season

Our broad jumpers run and jump a great deal. The major part of their work is repeat running on the track. They do repeat sprints of 60 to 80 yards, with easy jogging in between, and they often stride 110's, 220's and even 330's with the sprinters.

During competition season workouts, our broad jumpers never jump for distance. Jumping form is practiced with "short-run jumps," taking five to eight strides, hitting the board, and practicing form in the air. A boy can take 20 or 30 of these short-run jumps in one workout session, giving him plenty of opportunity to work on getting height, controlling his legs, and reaching for distance.

Before the Meet

The broad jumper's warmup before competition should be about the same as before practice sessions. He begins with variation running, such as high raising of the knees mixed with normal strides, and then goes through his calisthenics, being particularly careful to stretch the muscles and joints that are going to be put to use when he jumps. He finishes the warmup with some very fast sprints.

The amount of warmup needed is different with different athletes. Each of our boys uses an individualized warmup schedule which is developed according to his own needs. Each boy, in consultation with the coach, decides how much time he will put in on his exercises, how much effort will be put into it, and the amount of rest that he will take between the completion of his warmup and the start of competition.

A coach must try to develop the type of psychological atmosphere in which his athletes are ready for their event but not exhausted from having mentally competed over and over again. We often have meetings before competition and we usually discuss opponents. We not only have group sessions, but individual meetings as well, where we quietly preview the meet.

The coach can contribute quite a bit at these meetings. He must exert a quieting and educational influence and try to avoid the tendency to fire the boys up. They are usually more excited than the coach would like them to be as it is. The coach has to discuss matters pertaining to the meet, to opponents, and points to which the athletes should give last-minute attention, in such a way that they will profit from the discussion.

CHAPTER TEN

The Shot-Put

JESS MORTENSEN
University of Southern California

JESS MORTENSEN has posted an enviable record since 1951 when he became head coach at the University of Southern California. His Trojan teams have won six NCAA titles and have yet to lose a dual meet.

As an athlete at SC, Mortensen won two letters in football, was an All-Pacific Coast Conference cager, and won the NCAA and National AAU javelin titles. In 1931, while coaching at Riverside Junior College, Mortensen won the National Decathlon championship with a world-record-breaking score.

After 14 years at Riverside JC, Mortensen moved to the University of Denver as freshman football and head track coach. He turned out two unbeaten frosh grid teams and gave Denver its first Skyline Conference track championship.

Dean Cromwell, Mortensen's coach at Southern California, wrote in 1949 of "athletes who will give us marks that now seem fantastic," including the 60-foot shotput. * Mortensen has coached three such 60-footers at SC.

A member of the 1956 U. S. Olympic coaching staff, Mortensen is co-author of a popular track coaching book, *Track and Field for Coach and Athlete*. (Prentice-Hall, Inc., Englewood Cliffs, N. J., 1959.)

* Dean B. Cromwell and Al Wesson, *Championship Technique in Track and Field* (New York: McGraw-Hill Book Company, Inc., 1949), p. v.

The Shot-Put

For shot-put fans 1960 was a great year. Four men were breaking records week after week, preparing themselves for the showdown in early July when they would have to battle each other for the three Olympic team berths. Parry O'Brien's world record of 63-2, almost four years old, was still in the record books in the early part of the year; yet in less than one month, from March 5 to April 2, 1960, the world mark was improved five different times.

Dallas Long of the University of Southern California started the onslaught on March 5th when he threw 63-7 to break O'Brien's record. Two weeks later Bill Nieder pushed the record on up to 63-10. On the next weekend Dave Davis barely eclipsed Nieder's record with a 63-10½ effort, but Long, throwing in the same meet, came back to break the record again, this time throwing 64-6½. A week later Nieder again broke the world record when he threw 65-7. And to top it off, O'Brien himself bettered the world indoor record during that same month with a 62-5 toss.

In the Olympic Team Trials three months later, Long, O'Brien, and Davis * finished one-two-three to qualify for the Olympics in Rome, and Nieder, nursing an old knee injury, finished fourth. However, during the time between the trials and the team's departure for Rome, Davis developed a wrist injury and Nieder, as the alternate, was allowed to compete for the U.S.A. in place of Davis. Nieder

---

* EDITOR'S NOTE: All three were coached by Jess Mortensen at USC.

141

jumped at the chance to avenge his fourth place finish in the trials and came back to win the Olympic title and lead the United States to a sweep of the shot-put medals. O'Brien, two-time gold medal winner in this event, finished second. Long was third.

Physical Qualifications

With the great distances that are now being thrown, size has become almost essential in shot-putting. The top four finishers in the 1960 Olympic Trials ranged in size from 6-3 to 6-4 and in weight from 235 to 260. When looking for prospective putters, a coach will find that football linemen who are fast and well coordinated can often develop into good shot-putters.

Strength is also very important to the shot-putter. He must develop strength in his legs, back, arms and shoulders, and fingers. Of course, the best way to develop strength needed for shot-putting is through a thorough weight-lifting program.

Speed is another important factor in shot-putting. An increase in speed across the ring will cause an increase in the distance of the put. Parry O'Brien, Olympic champion in 1952 and 1956 and runner-up in 1960, was very fast on his feet. He even ran on one of the American sprint relay teams during a European tour. A big, strong boy who is not very fast may not be successful in this event.

The O'Brien Form

Parry O'Brien of the University of Southern California has been given credit for developing what is called the

O'Brien shot-putting form. (See Figure 21.) In the O'Brien form, the putter faces straight back away from the toe-board. This allows the putter to bend his body much lower over his right leg than previous putting forms. With a lower body position at the back of the circle, the putter is able to get a longer push on the shot. As the shot travelled across the ring in his hand, O'Brien was able to push against it 12 inches farther than had been possible with the previous styles. Of course, if force can be applied to the shot over a longer distance, the putter can put more force behind the shot and thus achieve greater distance.

Dallas Long uses the O'Brien form, too, as do most of the present-day putters, but because he has not been using it as long as O'Brien himself, Long's technique is not yet as good. He is young and will get stronger as his form improves. Barring injury, I think Long will reach the 70-foot mark before he is through.

The position at the back of the circle. The thrower stands at the back of the ring facing directly away from the direction of put.

The shot should be held well up in the fingers, resting against the putter's jaw and neck. (See Figure 22.) Each individual has his own way of holding the shot, but I think the best way is to have three fingers spread slightly behind the ball with the thumb and little finger helping to hold it so it will not slip off.

The glide across the circle. The putter dips low, keeping his weight well over his right leg. As he goes down, the left leg kicks up and across to start the push across the ring. The kick keeps the putter low and helps him accumulate speed across the circle.

His right foot lands in the center of the ring at an angle

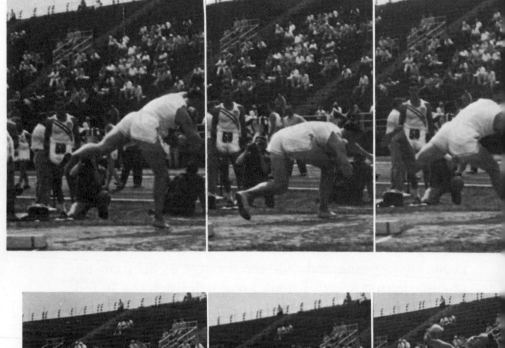

FIG. 21 **The O'Brien Shot-Putting Form.** Parry O'Brien of the University of Southern California, world record-holder and two-time Olympic champion, developed the O'Brien

form and became the first to ever throw 60 feet. Notice O'Brien's kick across the ring and the continuous movement of the shot in his hand. (Courtesy *Athletic Journal*)

FIG. 22

Holding the Shot. Dallas Long of the University of Southern California, NCAA shot put champion and world record holder, holds the shot well up in his fingers and rests it against his jaw and neck. (SC Photo)

of approximately 35 degrees, and the left foot is placed just to the left of the center of the toeboard. (See Figure 23.) Coaches who begin teaching the O'Brien form often assume that the right foot should face straight back when it lands in the middle of the ring, since it is in that position at the back of the circle. But it is almost impossible to put when the right foot is faced directly away from the direction of put.

It is important that the putter place his left foot no more than three or four inches to the left of the center of the toeboard. If it is placed too far to the left, the putter will open his hips and will not get the full value of the upward leg drive.

As the putter moves across the ring, the shot must travel in his hand in one continuous motion. One of the most common faults among shot-putters is stopping the shot momentarily in the middle of the circle in order to cock the arm for the putting action. Of course, stopping a 12- or 16-pound ball in motion and then starting it again is a waste of energy. The putter must keep the shot moving without hesitation until it is released.

The position at the front of the circle. When the right foot lands in the center of the circle and the left is next to the toeboard, the putter's weight is still over his right leg. Then as he begins the lift with his right leg and back, his hips and shoulders rotate to the left, his weight is shifted from his right leg on up over his left, and the shot is thrust up and out at an approximate angle of 45 degrees.

The arm should be fully extended at this point so that the shoulder, elbow, and hand are all in a straight line. The putter then follows through and reverses feet to help keep his balance at the conclusion of the put.

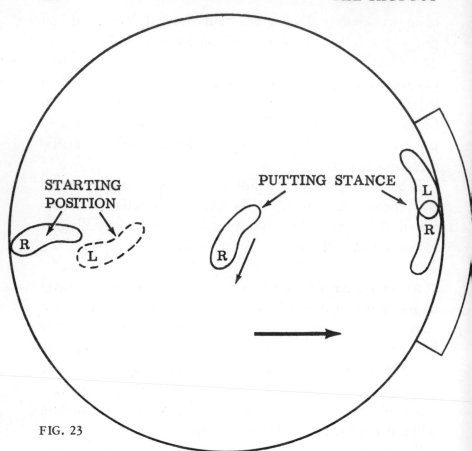

STARTING POSITION

PUTTING STANCE

FIG. 23

Foot   Placement   for   the   O'Brien   Shot- Putting Form

Working on form. During practice the coach cannot discover the errors a putter might be making by watching his general technique. He must watch specific elements of the putter's technique in order to pick out his mistakes.

Pictures can be an invaluable aid to the coach. We take slow motion movies of our putters and use them to help pick out any errors in form. With movies a coach can show an individual—more easily than he can tell him—what he is doing wrong and how he can improve.

Fouling

Fouling usually is brought about by poor balance, releasing the shot at too low an angle, getting too far over the left foot at the time of the put, or watching the shot in flight. O'Brien fell out of the ring and lost the NCAA title when he was a sophomore because he watched the shot until it landed on what would have been the winning throw.

Warmup

Before workouts, shot-putters must warm up properly to help eliminate the possibility of injuries. They should run a few wind sprints, and then do exercises that will stretch the muscles involved in putting. They should also do push-ups to warm up the arms and shoulders before beginning to throw.

Training Program *

Remember that it is impossible to judge whether each individual should follow any training plan to the letter. Allowances must be made for those who have a very heavy work and study program in school. Also, the age and maturity of each athlete should be considered. Some of the older, stronger men may need more work than most schedules contain. The coach and the athlete should determine the exact workout program that is needed. The schedule

---

* This program follows Mortensen and Cooper, *Track and Field for Coach and Athlete*, pp. 200-203.

presented below is suggested for the four weeks prior to participation in the first meet.

Workout Schedules

FOUR WEEKS PRIOR TO THE FIRST MEET

MONDAY:
1. Jog one-quarter mile.
2. Run wind sprints for half a mile—sprinting 50 yards and walking 50 yards.
3. Do stretching exercises involving the large muscles of the back and shoulders.
4. Do 10 pushups (repeated three times) executed from the fingertip position.
5. Do 20 puts from a standing position, concentrating on leg lift and proper delivery.
6. Do 20 to 30 puts by gliding across the ring and concentrating on form. Remember, the shot should be carried low in the hand for the first four weeks.
7. Take 6 to 10 starts from the blocks, running 25 yards each time.

TUESDAY:
1. Jog one-quarter mile.
2. Run wind sprints for half a mile.
3. Do stretching exercises.
4. Do 10 pushups (repeated three times) from the fingertip position.
5. Put the shot 10 times from a standing position.
6. Do 10 to 20 puts using the whole circle. Work on proper form.
7. Take five starts from the blocks.
8. Lift weights (see weight-lifting program).

WEDNESDAY:
1. Jog one-quarter mile.
2. Run wind sprints for half a mile.
3. Do stretching exercises.

4. Do 10 pushups (repeated three times) from fingertip position.
5. Put 10 times from a standing position.
6. Take 20 puts using the whole circle. Put hard enough to get proper timing, but not at an all-out effort for the first four weeks.
7. Execute a high jump at reasonable height, or a standing broad jump.

THURSDAY:
1. Jog one-quarter mile.
2. Run wind sprints for half a mile.
3. Do stretching exercises.
4. Take 10 puts from a standing position.
5. Do 10 to 20 puts across the circle.
6. Lift weights (*see* weight-lifting program).

FRIDAY:
1. Jog one-quarter mile.
2. Run wind sprints for half a mile.
3. Do stretching exercises.
4. Do 10 pushups (repeated three times) from the fingertip position.
5. Take 10 to 20 puts from a standing position.
6. Take 20 to 30 puts using the circle. Retrieve your own shot after each put; this gives you time to think about your faults and prepare for the next put.

SATURDAY:
Lift weights if time and facilities are available (*see* weight-lifting program).

After Meets Start

This schedule is set up in preparation for Saturday meets. When meets are held on Friday, the schedule should be altered accordingly.

MONDAY:
1. Jog one-quarter mile.
2. Run wind sprints for half a mile.

3. Do stretching exercises.
4. Do 10 pushups (repeated three times) from the fingertip position.
5. Take 10 puts from a standing position.
6. Take 15 to 25 puts using the whole circle.
7. Take 6 to 10 starts from the blocks, running 25 to 50 yards each time.
8. Check action pictures of your competition taken the previous Saturday.

TUESDAY:
1. Jog one-quarter mile.
2. Do stretching exercises.
3. Do five pushups (repeated three times) from the fingertip position.
4. Take 10 puts from a standing position.
5. Take 10 puts at all-out effort in competition with teammates.
6. Take six starts from the blocks, running 25 to 50 yards each time.

WEDNESDAY:
1. Jog one-quarter mile.
2. Run wind sprints for half a mile.
3. Do stretching exercises.
4. Do five pushups (repeated three times) from fingertip position.
5. Take 10 to 15 puts from a standing position.
6. Do 15 to 25 puts using the whole circle.
7. Lift weights (*see* weight-lifting program).

THURSDAY:
1. Jog one-quarter mile.
2. Run wind sprints for half a mile.
3. Do stretching exercises.
4. Do five pushups (repeated three times) from fingertip position.
5. Take 10 puts from a standing position.
6. Take seven puts under meet conditions.
7. Take six starts from the blocks, running 25 to 50 yards each time.

FRIDAY: Study motion pictures of yourself and others in action. Get plenty of sleep and rest. Prepare yourself mentally for a great performance on Saturday. Be confident!

SATURDAY: The day of track meet. Be prepared to compete at your best.
1. Arrive at the stadium in plenty of time to dress slowly and get properly warmed up for competition.
2. Jog one lap.
3. Do stretching exercises.
4. Take three starts, and run 25 yards each time.
5. Take 10 puts from a standing position.
6. Take five puts using the whole circle. Do not put with all-out effort. Try to time your action so that you are effective.
7. Do your best on each throw after competition begins. It is unwise to save up for any one all-out effort.

Weight-Lifting Program

The concept of using weights to improve performance in various events in track and field is a very recent development. For many years track coaches believed that lifting weights would make the athlete slow and "muscle-bound."

Most of the outstanding athletes of the past five years, however, have taken part in some type of weight-lifting. Especially is this true of the field events men.

Such outstanding performers as Bill Neider, Parry O'Brien, Dallas Long, and Dave Davis lifted weights regularly. It has been shown that weight-lifting may increase coordination, speed, or timing, and certainly will increase strength.

The weight-lifting program presented here is not considered to be a magic formula, nor is it designed to improve ability in any given event, but it may be used as one way to develop strength and coordination. Furthermore, tangible results cannot be obtained overnight. It takes time and consistent work under proper supervision to obtain the best results. The athlete preparing for a given track season should begin weight-lifting three times a week at least eight months before the season begins. During the competitive season it should be on a somewhat limited basis; that is, the lifting should be done only once or twice a week, depending on the strength and maturity of the performer. How far the athlete should increase the weight pounds as he progresses in his training depends upon many factors, the foremost being his strength and experience in weight-lifting. Other factors include his need for increased strength, the progress he has made, and the amount of time he devotes to this phase.

TWO-ARM EXERCISES *

A. Standing position
    1. *Two-arm barbell military press:*
       Do five sets of three to five repeats. The starting weight should be 70 to 100 pounds, but may be increased to 200 pounds. The lifting action should be done rapidly to help develop explosive power.
    2. *Two-arm barbell snatch:*
       Do three sets of five repeats starting with weight

---

* Adapted from:
Coker, Chuck, *Weight Training for Track and Field Athletes,* n.p., n.d.
Chandler, Otis, *Scientific Weightlifting Exercises Designed for Track and Field Events,* n.p., n.d.

from 70 to 100 pounds. The weight may be increased to 200 pounds. Make very quick lifts.
3. *Curls:*
Do three sets of five repeats.
4. *Deep knee bends (not more than 90-degree bend):*
Do three sets of five repeats, starting weight 70 to
150 pounds. The weight may be increased to 300
pounds. Do one set of five repeats, jumping off the
floor with the weights. Be careful to bend the knees
only to the position where the thighs are parallel
to the floor.
5. *Dumbbell military press (one arm):*
(a) Do three sets of eight repeats, starting weight
20 to 40 pounds.
(b) Start the action in a shot-putting stance, using
the legs, back, and arm in same manner as
when putting the shot from a standing position.
6. *Wrist and finger curls:*
Do three or five repeats, starting weight 70 to 100
pounds.
B. Prone position
Two-arm barbell prone press on a bench:
Do three sets of 10 repeats, starting weight 70 to 100
pounds. The weight may be increased to 250 pounds.

Injuries

In putting the shot, fingers and tendons of the hand and
wrist are more often injured than any other part of the
body. Many shot-putters increase the possibility of injury
by carrying the shot high in the fingers. By means of
weight-lifting and other similar exercises, putters can build
up tremendous strength in the back, shoulders and arms,
but it is more difficult for them to strengthen the fingers,
hands and wrists; consequently these are often neglected.
Exercises such as pushups from the fingertips as well as

wrist and finger curls with weights should be included in the training program to help prevent such injuries.

Before the Meet

Our shot-putters get out on the field about 30 minutes before the meet is to start to begin their warmup. They do their jogging and their stretching exercises, take a few easy throws from a standing position, and then throw five hard ones from the ring.

Some putters throw all-out during their warmup in an effort to get off a good practice throw and "psych" opponents. Psychology can be a factor in shot-putting, as in any event, but it is a mistake to use energy trying to upset an opponent before the competition begins. This energy could be put to much better use in competition.

CHAPTER ELEVEN

The Discus Throw

JIM KELLY
University of Minnesota

JIM KELLY has had a long, successful career in track and field. Since 1937 when he became head coach at the University of Minnesota, he has developed a number of great athletes, including his two world-record-breaking discus throwers, Bob Fitch and Fortune Gordien.

Kelly's Minnesota athletes have won the NCAA title (1948) and one Big Ten outdoor championship (1949). His Gopher tracksters have won 23 Big Ten and six NCAA individual titles.

In addition to his coaching duties at Minnesota, Kelly was head coach of the 1951 United States track and field team in the Pan-American Games in Buenos Aires, head coach of the 1956 U. S. Olympic team in Melbourne, and assistant coach of the 1959 U. S. team in the U.S.A.-U.S.S.R. dual meet.

For his outstanding job as coach of the 1956 Olympic squad, Kelly received the *Los Angeles Times* Award for outstanding coaching, The Knute Rockne "Coach of the Year" award, and the Western Airlines plaque for the "Outstanding Contribution to Track, 1956." Kelly also is a member of the Helms Foundation Hall of Fame.

The Discus Throw

One of the developers of the Minnesota style of discus throwing, which consists of a 1¾ turn and hop, emphasizing speed across the ring, was Bob Fitch of the University of Minnesota. His world record of 180-2¾ was set in 1946 and stood for 2½ years.

Fortune Gordien of Minnesota, improving slightly upon Fitch's style, broke the world record in 1949 with a throw of 186-11 and then improved his own world record in 1953 with a throw of 194-6. This stood until 1959.

Other Minnesota discus throwers have used this same style with success, too. Byrl Thompson threw 174 feet, Dale Yonkey threw 171, and both Jerry Helgeson and Charles Lindekugel had throws of over 160 feet.

At the time the Minnesota style was developed, competitors from a few other schools were throwing with the 1¾ turn, too, but they were stepping straight across the ring. We wanted to get more momentum from the turn; therefore we had our throwers begin their hop from the left foot near the back of the circle to the right foot past the center of the circle, thus giving them more room to turn than any throwers had ever had before.

Physical Qualifications

To become a great discus thrower, a boy has to have a good, explosive arm. The coach can teach him form, but the boy must have a throwing arm that is strong and quick.

159

Through practice a boy's arm is built up, just as it is in baseball. It gets stronger as he continues his throwing.

Size and height mean a lot, too. Most discus throwers are also football players—big, agile men. Fitch and Gordien, however, were not as big as the best throwers of today. Fitch stood 6-2; Gordien was slightly over six feet tall; both weighed just under 200 pounds at the peak of their throwing careers.

Al Oerter, the 1956 and 1960 Olympic champion, was 6-3 and weighed 235. Rink Babka and Dick Cochran, the second and third place finishers in the 1960 games, stood 6-5 each. Babka weighed 267 and Cochran 225.

The thrower also has an added advantage if he has long arms. The longer the arms the better, as long as they are not out of proportion with the rest of his body.

Controlled speed has become necessary for discus throwers. The momentum of a fast turn will add greatly to the distance of a throw. Fitch and Gordien were both rather fast on their feet and both were extremely fast across the ring.

Proper Form

When starting a discus thrower, first teach him to sail the discus correctly. All sailing is done from a standing position without the turn. The beginning discus thrower should get the feel of the discus by sailing it easily again and again. Then, after he works up to where the sailing is pretty smooth, a little more snap and explosive action can be put into it.

The discus should rest on the thrower's open hand with

his first three fingers hooked over the edge of the discus at their first joint. The thrower's palm is down, and the discus rolls off the index finger of his throwing hand spinning clockwise as it sails.

The position of the discus in the air is controlled by the hand. A wobbly discus can be corrected by working on sailing. A wobble is often brought about by putting too much force behind the throw.

The thrower's arm, fully extended, is brought up "through the shoulder" at an approximate angle of 40 degrees, and the discus is released at shoulder height. (See Figure 24.) If he throws either over or under the plane of his shoulder, he will not be able to get as much distance. As his body is coming around, the thrower's wrist has to be in extension. His wrist must be straight as the discus rolls off his forefinger and begins its flight.

When the discus leaves the thrower's hand, he follows through by reversing feet. The reversing is not actually part of the throw, but it is a necessary part of discus throwing. It keeps the thrower in balance and reduces the possibility of fouling. A boy who throws without reversing has held back something.

All discus throwers are a little awkward when they first begin to turn as they throw, and it usually takes quite a while to get them to turn as smoothly as they should. The value of the turn cannot be overemphasized. Only when he gets to the point where the turn is no problem to him can a boy concentrate on the discus itself.

The right-handed discus thrower pivots on his left foot, hops beyond the middle of the ring to his right foot, steps to the front of the ring with his left, throws, and changes

FIG. 24   **Releasing the Discus.** Bob Fitch of the University of Minnesota, world record holder in the discus throw, brings his
arm, fully extended, up "through the shoulder" at an approximate angle of 40 degrees. (Photo: University of Minnesota)

feet. (See Figure 25.) Of course, the whole procedure is exactly reversed for left-handed throwers. It's hop, drive, throw, and reverse.

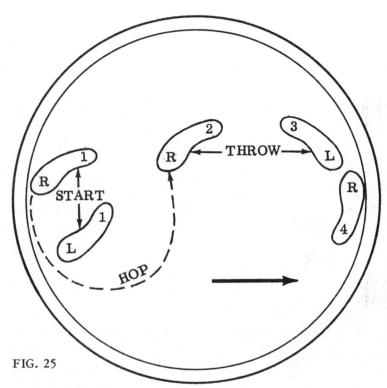

FIG. 25

Footwork Used in the Minnesota Style of Discus Throwing

In the turn, the boy must be taught to keep his balance. The turn cannot be made properly when the thrower is in an erect position. Yet he must not lean over too far or he will lose his balance and be in an unfavorable position for the throw after completing his turn.

The boy has to be down and in balance at the same time. His knees and trunk are bent so that his hips will travel through a wider arc, giving the body greater momentum in the turn. His center of gravity should be kept well ahead of the feet so that the upper body and hips lead the turn.

During the preliminary windup the thrower stands with his back toward the direction of the throw and with his right foot hops around his left leg to a point past the center of the circle. (See Figure 26.) Then the left foot continues around and is placed at the front edge of the circle. He then executes the leg drive and hip pivot, which add considerable power to the throw. As the left foot is planted at the front of the circle, the thrower's knees are still slightly bent and he faces to the side about 90 degrees from the line of flight of the discus. He then drives upward with his legs by straightening them. At the same time, he forcefully pivots his hips around so that he is facing forward toward the line of flight and is standing erect. During the entire turn and up to this point, the discus has been held back as far as is conveniently possible. (Holding back the discus with fully extended arm until the moment of the actual throw permits greater acceleration of the discus by allowing the longest possible arc through which to whip the discus during the throwing motion.)

Now the throw is made. As the discus is swung forcefully around and up through shoulder level, the thrower shifts his weight from his right leg to his straight left leg. Locking the left leg helps prevent fouling. After throwing, the thrower reverses his feet as he follows through and keeps his eye on the discus as it sails away from him.

A problem with the beginner is getting him to hop past the center of the circle instead of to the center. The hop past the center gives more room for the turn and therefore allows the athlete to put more power into the throw.

Discus throwers should not develop the habit of stopping in their throw before making the delivery. It is very common to see boys stop during their throws so that the turn is not a smooth, continuous motion into the follow-through. If they hop and stop, they have lost the benefit of the turn-momentum.

To keep a boy from fouling, work on turning and on keeping in balance. Much of this can be accomplished while teaching the boy to sail the discus properly, for at that time it is easier to see what he is doing wrong.

Pre-Season

We have always done some weight training. We had our boys lifting weights long before this became an accepted practice, but we have never done it to the extent that some do now. The boys go to the weight room regularly during the winter, but they do very little lifting after competition starts in the spring.

Since most discus throwers play football in the fall, our pre-season work begins in the winter. We have always had a fieldhouse with enough room for throwing the discus, and that is where we do a lot of our work.

Workouts consist mostly of throwing the discus. After the boys do the standard bending and stretching exercises and quite a few pushups, they sail the discus 20 to 25 times, stepping forward with the left foot, sailing the discus up through the shoulder, and reversing feet. They must never throw without that follow-through.

Discus throwers should throw from the ring a lot, too, so that they do not get in the habit of fouling. The more room a boy has for the turn, the farther he will be able to throw, so it is natural for him to want to take more room when his

FIG. 26

The Discus Throw. Fortune Gordien of the University of
Minnesota, world record holder and three-time Olympic
team member, demonstrates the Minnesota style of discus

throwing. Notice his distinct hop as he leaves the ground with both feet and lands beyond the center of the circle with his right foot. (Courtesy *Scholastic Coach*)

turn is not confined to that 8-2 circle. Years ago, discus throwers were even more confined than they are now. The ring was only seven feet across, and this is one of the reasons the marks were no better than they were at that time.

A coach should spend quite a bit of time with discus throwers, particularly when they are first learning. But even when a boy gets to the point where he is throwing the discus great distances, he has to be well trained. A boy who is throwing 135 feet may begin doing something wrong and drop off only a few feet. But a boy throwing 180 to 190 feet who develops a hitch in his throwing can lose 10 or 15 feet in a hurry.

When Fitch was developing, he had a job in the afternoons and worked out at lunchtime. I would spend those 35 to 40 minutes a day watching his throw and follow-through, looking for the things that he should concentrate on. I tried to develop him slowly. I don't believe a coach should try to teach a boy everything at once.

Discus throwers should be watched from every angle with little suggestions made after every throw. Some boys, especially the beginners, want someone to give them a lot of help. With other boys a coach can just drop by once in a while to make suggestions and then go away to let them work it out. If a boy is a little jittery, he will often do better if the coach isn't standing over him.

During the Season

A problem with most discus throwers is that they are fascinated by their event. I don't know of any athletes that are more dedicated than discus throwers. Rather than getting the boys to throw enough, often the problem is keeping them from throwing too much. They love to throw that discus and they will throw for long periods of time if allowed to. The coach must sell his throwers on resting the last couple of days before competition.

Our boys work out the first three days of every week. They do their stretching exercises and pushups first and then sail the discus a few times. The throwing of the discus takes care of the upper body, but the legs have to be in good shape, too, and that is best accomplished through running. Our discus throwers usually get in their running with the sprinters.

During the workout, the boys take 30 to 40 throws from the ring, but these are not always hard throws. The best distances often come when the boys are not trying to overpower their throw.

The boys should not spend too much time in the ring just before each throw. They should step in, swing the discus back and forth a couple of times, and then go right into the turn.

You have to guard against the boys' getting blisters on their fingers. If the discus is being thrown properly, this is the only injury common to discus throwers. Rough edges and nicks should be filed off the discus or should be marked so it can be adjusted in the thrower's hand.

On Thursdays the boys do not throw at all. They may come out and run a little, but they need to store up energy in that arm so that it will have the needed snap on the day of competition.

There is no workout on the day before competition, but the boys do come out and loosen up the day after.

Before the Meet

Our boys eat steak, roast beef, or eggs four hours before competition. Regarding sleep, any athlete can use plenty, of course, but I think it is especially important that he gets a good night's sleep two nights before the meet.

The warmup for competition is the same as in practice. Our throwers like to get out almost an hour before competition and begin to do their running and stretching exercises. Then they sail the discus several times and take a few throws from the ring. They like to sail it, too, while waiting their next turn to throw.

Our boys do not take dextrose or any other quick-energy producer before competing. The less you go in for fads, the less chance there is of upsetting the boys if they have to go without these things.

In the discus throw, the coach can teach a boy how to compete. It's a sort of intangible thing, but it can be done by talking to him. Relaxation and control must be stressed. Some boys throw well in practice, but don't do well in meets. They have to be taught to relax and throw as they always do. When a discus thrower tries too hard, chances are he will tie up and throw poorly. If his throw is smooth and relaxed, he probably will have a good performance.

CHAPTER TWELVE

Cross-Country

F. X. CRETZMEYER
State University of Iowa

F. X. CRETZMEYER, track coach at the University of Iowa since 1948, has developed a number of great cross-country runners, including three who became Olympic distance runners. Rich Ferguson, twice Big Ten cross-country champion, competed in the 1952 Olympics. Deacon Jones, National Collegiate cross-country champion, was a member of both the 1956 and 1960 Olympic teams. Ted Wheeler, who ran second to Ferguson and Jones in cross-country, but won four Big Ten 880 and mile titles, ran on the 1956 Olympic team.

Since Cretzmeyer's return to Iowa where he starred in track and field, his runners have broken eight of 12 Iowa indoor records and have bettered 16 and tied three outdoor marks. One record his athletes have not been able to hurdle, however, is held by Cretzmeyer himself. He scored a total of 144½ points during the 1936 season.

A recognized leader in the field, Cretzmeyer is co-author of a highly regarded track coaching book, *Track and Field Athletics*. (The Mosby Company, St. Louis.) On the market since 1937, it is now in its fifth edition.

Cretzmeyer was honored recently by being elected president of the National Cross-Country Coaches Association.

Cross-Country

To be a cross-country runner a boy has to be strong—both physically and mentally. Long-distance running is strenuous exercise but is very good for boys, and most of them learn to like it. They have to like it to become very good at it.

All distance running requires great determination. The athlete who wants to become a good cross-country runner must be willing to withstand the feeling of fatigue, which is often largely psychological. A boy has to convince himself that his opponents are just as tired as he is.

Running Form

The cross-country runner must run relaxed so that he uses as little energy as possible throughout the race. Each stride is easy and natural.

Relaxation comes about more readily when the arms are held higher than for the shorter races. The arms are carried in a rolling motion rather than a mechanical action as they swing. (See Figure 27.)

When running downhill, the runner plants his heel first and relaxes as his momentum carries him along. Going uphill, he uses his arms vigorously and works to maintain his running speed. The runner also should bend his knees and shorten his stride a little to facilitate uphill running.

FIG. 27 **Stride and Arm Action.** Ted Wheeler, an outstanding cross-country runner at the State University of
Iowa, winner of four Big Ten distance champion-

ships and member of the 1956 Olympic team, runs
with an easy, natural stride. Notice the rolling motion of his arms. (Courtesy *Athletic Journal*)

Workouts

Our runners begin their warmup with easy jogging and a few speed bursts before beginning their bending and stretching exercises. Warmup is an individual proposition. Each boy experiments with various methods of warming up early in the year and through his own experience will know how much warmup he needs. Of course, on a cold day more exercising is necessary to prepare the athlete for running than on a warm day. Many times the first part of the race can be used as the final stages of the warmup.

Our cross-country practices are held five days a week, Sunday through Thursday. During midseason, the week's work might be as follows:

SUNDAY—Everyone does some easy running. There is no set amount of work that the boys are required to do. Just long, easy running with some sprints at the end of the workout.

MONDAY—The boys go out on the golf course and fartlek, trying to get in six to eight miles of running. As the boys begin running in a pack, they will try to stay together, but of course the better runners get away from the poorer ones. If they follow the same route every day, the boy who has to drop behind all the time will begin to lose his enthusiasm. To keep the slower runners from getting discouraged, they can cut across the course and catch up whenever they begin to drop back very far.

At the end of the workout, the better runners may have run for an hour or an hour and a half and covered seven or eight miles. The slower boys have run for the same period of time, but they may have run only six miles. Everyone gets the same amount of running time but does not necessarily cover the same amount of distance. This gives the team more of a feeling of "togetherness."

Occasionally, the boys run Indian file and have the last man keep moving up to take the lead and set the pace as they run. When they do this, each boy has to accelerate each time he moves up.

TUESDAY—The boys do a lot of repetitions. We have a 440-yard straight-away marked off on the golf course where the boys can pace through repeat quarters. They may do 15 to 20 of them, gradually increasing the pace throughout the season until they are running them in 68 to 70 seconds. They jog back slowly, each week cutting down on the time they take for the jog, and then run down the straight-away again.

Sometimes instead of quarters they will run half miles, hitting them in 2:20 or 2:30. The idea is to keep the pace steady and try to run about a five-minute mile.

WEDNESDAY—Again, pace is emphasized. The boys usually run repeat miles or two-miles. Once in a while they will run a three-mile, rest 10 minutes, and then run a mile or two-mile.

THURSDAY—We begin to lighten the load. The boys may run repeat quarters or halves on the track, working on pace. We try to work on the track once a week.

FRIDAY—No practice.

SATURDAY—Competition.

The boys finish every workout with some sprinting work. Although he is tired, a boy must be a sprinter when he finishes a cross-country race. He must go into a sprint where the action is rather mechanical, picking up his knees and swinging his arms vigorously. Our course has a steep hill that is about 180 yards long where we often finish practice with three or four uphill sprints.

So that workouts do not become a drudgery, we try to vary the practice schedules as much as possible. Once in a while we will divide the team into two groups and have them run in opposite directions around the course. When the groups meet, they turn around and go back. The better runners get more work that way.

For added variety, we have a workout we call the "Four-Minute Mile." The boys have 10 minutes in which to run a four-minute mile, using 220's, quarters, halves, or any combination of these.

To run a four-minute mile using 220's, the runner must run eight 220's, averaging 30 seconds, with a 51-second rest between each of them. With quarters, the runner has to average 60 seconds for four 440's with a two-minute rest between them. Using halves, a boy can run 2:00, rest six minutes, and then must run another 880 in 2:00.

In the four-minute mile workout, 220's are the easiest and halves are the hardest. For high school runners it might be better to give the boys 15 minutes to complete the workout rather than 10, giving them a little longer rest between races.

Our distance runners lift weights twice a week, concentrating on developing the upper body but also working on the legs. Boys build up their legs automatically when they walk and run, but they must do weight exercises to develop strength in their arms and shoulders. Our exercises consist of the usual lifts as well as pushups and chins.

Fartlek System of Training

Fartlek, meaning "speed-play" in Swedish, consists of acquiring physical conditioning through a special program of running. The athlete alternates his pace between running, walking, and quick bursts of speed over a cross-country course. The distances and speeds used depend upon the ability and physical condition of the individual runner.

A sample practice schedule * is as follows:

1. Warm up by running easily for 5 to 10 minutes.
2. Run at a fast, steady speed over a distance of ¾ to 1¼ miles.
3. Walk rapidly for five minutes.
4. Practice easy running, broken by sprints of 65 to 75 yards, repeating until fatigue becomes evident.
5. Run easily, injecting three or four swift steps occasionally.
6. Run at full speed uphill for 175 to 200 yards.
7. Run at a fast pace for one minute.
8. Finish the routine by running one to five laps around the track, depending on the distance run in competition.

Before the Meet

Most competitors are a little jumpy and have trouble sleeping the night before a race, so we tell them to try to get a good night's sleep two nights before.

Cross-country runners should eat at least four hours be-

---

* George T. Bresnahan, W. W. Tuttle and Francis X. Cretzmeyer, *Track and Field Athletics* (St. Louis: The C. V. Mosby Company, 1956), p. 48.

FIG. 28 **Two of Coach Cretzmeyer's Great Cross-Country Runners**—Rich Ferguson, twice Big Ten cross-country
champion and member of the 1952 Canadian Olympic

team, and Deacon Jones, national cross-country champion and member of both the 1956 and 1960 U. S. Olympic teams. (Photo: State University of Iowa)

fore a race. But when a meet is run at 10 in the morning, as many of them are, we get up at six and eat as soon as we can so the food will be pretty well digested by racetime.

Warming up before the meet is about the same as before practice, but if the boys are going to be running a course that is strange to them, they will go around the course for part of the warmup. If the race is on our course and the other team is not familiar with it, our boys will show them around.

Between the warmup and the race, the runners should try to rest for 10 minutes or so. It is especially relaxing for them to lie down, put their feet up and untie their shoes.

The Race

Cross-country is quite a team sport. It is possible to have a runner win the race and still have your team get trounced. Even the "tail-enders" can help. A team's sixth and seventh runners can add points to the score of their team if they come in before the other team's fifth man finishes.

Having the team run together for part of the race will sometimes help pull the slower boys along. Occasionally, during a race, the better runners can talk the slower boys into doing better.

Once in a while a runner will get way behind during a race and then come sprinting in at the end when it is too late. I tell a boy who does that that I would rather have him stick with his teammates for half or three-quarters of a race, and even drop out if he has to, then to lag behind and then sprint in when it doesn't do any good.

When running uphill, runners have a tendency to let up

after reaching the top. We have won meets by telling our boys to keep accelerating for 100 to 150 yards after they have reached the top of a hill. Accelerating in this way often causes members of the other team to fall behind and get discouraged.

When we have a meet on our own course, our boys plan in advance the pace they are going to run. They try to go by the miles and half miles in the time that has been decided, but it must be within reason. Each week the boys try to bring down the time a little.

Injuries

Cross-country runners have to take good care of their feet. We try to prevent blisters by making sure each boy's shoes fit properly and by toughening the feet with benzoin.

Since their arches take quite a beating during long races, the boys do foot exercises. They pick up marbles with their toes or wad up a towel under their feet with their toes. Both of these exercises help to strengthen arches.

Sometimes a runner may get a stitch (a pain in his side). The best way to alleviate the pain is to run it out. If the boy makes up his mind that he is going to continue running and get rid of the stitch, the pain will often subside.

Is Long-Distance Running Injurious to Health?

Many people believe that distance running is harmful to the heart and will shorten the life span of those who run long distances. Statistics show, however, that cross-country runners live as long as or longer than those who do not participate in distance running.

According to Bresnahan, Tuttle and Cretzmeyer,* Jones and Best of the University of Wisconsin report that, over a period of 48 years, 171 individuals have been awarded major letters in cross-country running. Of this number of athletes, two have died from accidental causes and seven from unspecified causes. As compared with similar groups, the athletes participating in endurance events seem to have a slight advantage over those who do not take part in such exercise.

Distance running is not harmful to boys as long as they are physically fit and follow a sensible conditioning program. Every boy should have a thorough physical examination before he is allowed to run and then should be trained so that his workout sessions become gradually more strenuous.

---

* Bresnahan, Tuttle and Cretzmeyer, *Track and Field Athletics*, p. 146.

EDITOR'S NOTE: Besides the obvious advantages for distance runners who compete in cross-country, it has also been mentioned as an aid in teaching relaxation and in developing leg spring for other events. (See Chapters 1 and 7.)

A. Muscles and Strength

IRVING L. KINTISCH
Assistant Track Coach
Manhattan College

B. Resistance Exercises
for Track and Field

JIM MURRAY
and PETER V. KARPOVICH

Appendix

A. MUSCLES AND STRENGTH

By Irving L. Kintisch, Assistant Track Coach, Manhattan College.
(Reprinted, with minor changes, by permission of the author and
Scholastic Coach.)

Strength plays a vital role in the success of participants in track and field. The stronger the athlete, the better are his chances for success—all other things being equal. A trend which has rapidly mushroomed is the use of weights to develop strength. Some track coaches have been reluctant to accept this concept, and it is hoped that this article will crystallize their thinking.

To understand how strength in a muscle may develop, it is important to first understand the structure of muscle.

About 75 of some 200 pairs of muscles in the body concern themselves with the maintenance of posture and locomotion. These muscles vary in size and shape. Each is composed of thread-like fibers, the number of fibers varying from six to several hundred thousand.

The muscle cells are long and very narrow, hence the term fiber. Each fiber is ensheathed by a delicate membrane called a sarcolemma. These fibers are massed together in bundles which in turn are bound together into large masses.

Work is done by the muscle when it changes form by shortening. As each muscle fiber shortens, it swells out laterally. The sarcolemma and the connective tissues surrounding the fibers become stretched, thereby making it

187

hard to the touch. Heavy muscular work done with some degree of regularity will tend to thicken and toughen the sarcolemma.

It is an accepted physiological fact that muscles will increase in size and strength with regular and strenuous exercise. It is necessary for a muscle to work close to its capacity load in order to develop in strength.

What actually occurs is that unused fibers or fibers that are small because of little use are brought into play. They develop due to the increased demand placed upon them. The amount of strength to be gained will be limited by the athlete's anatomical structure.

Every physiologist agrees that in order to develop additional strength, the exercise must be conducted against increased weight resistance. As the amount of weight resistance that can be overcome increases, so does the strength. Mere repetitions of the exercise will increase endurance but not strength. Through training, an athlete can develop the strength to lift heavier and heavier weights.

Every athlete will admit to doing at least a minimum amount of certain strenuous exercises to develop strength for his particular event. They will perform pushups, chins, dips on parallel bars, rope-climbing, sit-ups, and any number of favorite strenuous activities designed to build strength.

What they are doing is adding resistance to a muscular movement which for the most part is limited to all or part of the body's weight. The value in barbells lies in providing additional resistance beyond the body weight as the need for more strength arises.

Coaches opposed to weight training contend that the

athlete often becomes musclebound and loses his speed. Ken Doherty, former head coach at the University of Pennsylvania, believes that a relationship between strength and speed probably does exist. In his book, *Modern Track and Field*,* he writes, "To get a heavy object, such as a 16-pound shot, in motion as quickly as possible, obviously requires strength and quickness of action—the heavier the object, the more strength is needed; the lighter it is, the more speed." I believe an explanation of this is necessary to show that strength and speed are more closely related than many coaches are ready to admit.

The weight of the 16-pound shot provides enough resistance for the great majority of collegiate shot-putters to slow down the muscle contractions involved in putting. The 12-pound shot is heavy enough to do the same for the great majority of high school putters.

The athlete works to achieve greater strength. This added strength allows him to overcome the weight resistance and makes for a quicker muscular contraction, thereby increasing the momentum of the shot as it leaves the hand. *The additional strength has made the athlete faster.*

It is recommended that the weight-lifting practices be done on alternate days. If lifting is done each day, muscle soreness will develop. Lifting should be done with quickness of movement in mind. Rapidity of movement against the weight's resistance is important. Repeat each movement a minimum of five times and a maximum of 10. When the movement can be repeated more than 10 times, the resistance should be increased by adding weight. Re-

---

* Doherty, Ken: *Modern Track and Field* (Englewood Cliffs, N.J.: Prentice-Hall, Inc., 1953.)

member, repetitions will develop endurance, exercising will develop strength.

In handling heavy weights, be careful of technique. Injury might occur when a heavy weight is lifted improperly. Feet should be spread shoulder-width for most lifts.

A precautionary word is necessary here. *Weight-lifting should never replace training for the event itself.* The athlete must still dedicate himself to the almost endless task of developing the skills and coordinations so necessary for success. It is the combination of this skill plus the added strength that may make the mediocre performers of today the champions or near-champions of tomorrow.

B. RESISTANCE EXERCISES FOR TRACK AND FIELD

Jim Murray and Peter V. Karpovich, *Weight Training in Athletics* (Englewood Cliffs, N.J.: Prentice-Hall, Inc., 1956), Chap. 11. Reprinted with Permission.

It is in track and field that much experimentation with weight training has been done by top-ranking competitors. Men like Bob Richards, Mal Whitfield, Otis Chandler, Parry O'Brien, Fortune Gordien, and Bob Backus have shown that weight training can be a positive asset to runners, jumpers, and throwers alike.

Having won top honors in pole vaulting at the Olympics, and United States championships in the Decathlon and All-Around, Bob Richards is an outstanding example of a man that can lift weights and be an enduring, fast-moving, and superbly coordinated athlete. He began practicing standard weight-lifting exercises while 12 years of age and was outstanding at basketball and football before specializing in track and field.

Richards practiced little weight-training exercise for his

legs, fearing that to do so would result in increased muscle size, the weight of which would handicap his vaulting. He did work his legs with an extension movement, using weights attached to his feet, especially on one occasion when he was hospitalized for an appendectomy prior to the 1948 Olympiad. He credits this exercise, plus the pressing of a barbell while lying supine in his hospital bed, with enabling him to resume hard training after his convalescence with the result that he made the U. S. Olympic team. In his regular training program, Richards prepared for the pole vault as follows:

1. Approximately 30 vaults.
2. Five to ten 60-yard wind sprints.
3. Rope-climbing.
4. 15 to 20 minutes of weight training.
5. Freehand exercises and gymnastics, such as chinning, and press-ups into the handstand position.

The specific weight training movements Richards used were the clean and press, the curl, the reverse curl, the pullover, and leg-raises with 5-pound weights attached to each foot. Richards practiced pressing in decreasing repetitions, starting with five with 135 pounds, and cutting the repetitions gradually as he worked up in weight to a single press with 160 pounds. His curls were done with about 70 pounds for six to ten repetitions. These exercises developed strength for pulling up on the pole and pushing off to clear the crossbar. The leg-raising movement, in which Richards did 10 to 20 repetitions, is one which contributes to both abdominal and thigh strength.

Incidentally, Richards occasionally added variety to his weight-training program by practicing the lifts used in competition. On one occasion, he made a dozen single cleans and jerks with 225 pounds. This lift requires, and conversely develops, all-around coordinated strength and great explosive power. Richards' lifts, made at a weight of approximately 160 pounds, would have rated him a worthy contender for middleweight honors in smaller AAU district weight-lifting contests. Richards' best performances in track and field events, at the time he was practicing the above weight-training exercises, were as follows: 100-meter dash, 10.9 seconds; broad jump, 23 feet; 16-pound shot-put, 43 feet; high jump, 6-1; 400-meter run, 51.6 seconds; 110-meter high hurdles, 15.2 seconds; javelin throw, 196 feet; pole vault, 15-4¾; 1500-meter run, 4:51.0; discus throw, 136 feet.

Mal Whitfield's approach to weight training seems at first surprising, but is logical upon investigation. In view of his great ability at various distances, it is worth careful consideration. Whitfield, two-time Olympic Games 800-meter running champion, felt that his practice on the track provided him with all the endurance he needed, so his weight training was designed to produce maximum strength by using heavy weights and low repetitions.

Whitfield did his barbell/dumbbell exercises in sets of five or three repetitions, using incredible poundages for a 6-1 middle-distance runner weighing 170 pounds. He practiced full squats in five sets of three repetitions, a total of 15 squats, with the barbell loaded to 225 to 270 pounds. Other exercises included bent-arm pullovers (again using heavy weights, to 250 pounds), straight-arm pullovers, overhead presses, supine presses, and sit-ups with feet elevated on an incline while holding 25 pounds behind his head. Two exercises that were special favorites were the one-legged squat (alternating legs for five repetitions) while holding 50 to 75 pounds, and an arm-swinging movement, similar to the action of running (practiced in running stance) while holding 10- to 25-pound dumbbells in each hand.

It should be emphasized, however, that Whitfield did not continue this strenuous weight training through the track season, but discontinued it when he began running competitively. With him, weight training was an out-of-season conditioner.

For runners and jumpers the following exercises are recommended:

Runners and Hurdlers

1. Clean and press, 10 repetitions.
2. Squat, three repetitions, five sets.
3. Pullover, 10 repetitions with light weight after each set of squats.
4. Curl, 10 repetitions.

Jumpers

This is same as runner's program, but with the addition of *quick* partial bends with heavier weights on shoulders, 10 repetitions, three sets. The knee-dip should be to no more than one-quarter squat position, flat-footed, and with body erect. This exercise should be practiced after the full knee bend.

Pole Vaulters

1. Clean and press, light weight, 10 repetitions.
2. Heavy press, three repetitions, four sets.
3. Curl, eight repetitions, two sets.

4. Reverse curl (knuckles up), eight repetitions, two sets.
5. Partial knee bends (see jumpers' program).
6. Pullover, 10 repetitions after each set of partial squats.
7. Leg-raise, 15 to 20 repetitions, preferably with a five-pound weight on each foot.

The programs advocated for track, and field events not classed as weight-throwing, are prescribed for use as out-of-season training. Of course, the runners and jumpers will want to continue some form of work on the track or road-work in the off-season as well. Vaulters should include some gymnastics, rope-climbing, and similar exercises. The weight-training movements should be done only three days per week, especially if the athlete is training at all strenuously on an indoor or outdoor track. Note the partial bend exercise recommended for jumpers and vaulters. This exercise will develop strength and spring over approximately the same range of action used in a take-off, and has the added advantage of being one which will produce strength without having much effect on muscle size. With Bob Richards' concern about body weight in mind, this is the only leg exercise listed for vaulters. Vaulters seeking additional leg strength, however, may experiment with the jumpers' leg program, meanwhile keeping a check on body weight. It is probable that athletes following a rigorous program, which includes considerable running, will not add weight appreciably to their legs even if they practice full squats.

Otis Chandler, one of the first men to put the 16-pound shot more than 57 feet, was an enthusiastic weight trainer (and competitive lifter) who made a study of the use of weights by track and field men. He learned that seven of the first 11 shot-putters to pass 56 feet used weight-training exercises, and was unable to obtain data on two. Chandler was of the opinion that the two who said they did not use weight training, Charles Fonville and Jim Fuchs, would have been better shot-putters if they had. Chandler recommended exercises like those listed for weight men and advocated standing leg-raises with weights on the feet for jumpers and runners.

For shot-putters, discus throwers, hammer throwers, and javelin throwers, it is suggested that at least one or two months be devoted to basic exercises of fundamental weight training. Men competing in the throwing events need all-around strength and will find that such strength will benefit them in whatever event they enter. Suggested preseason (one or two months before and up to the beginning of actual practice of the event) training is as follows:

Shot-Put

1. Clean and press, 10 repetitions, light weight.
2. Alternate press, heavy dumbbells; five repetitions with each hand, four sets.
3. Squat, five repetitions, four sets.
4. Pullover, 10 repetitions.
5. Sit-ups with weight behind head, twisting to touch elbows to opposite knees alternately, 20 repetitions.
6. Supine press, five repetitions, four sets.
   For the shot-putter the head end of the bend should be raised so that the angle at which the barbell is pressed is approximately the angle at which the shot is released.

Discus Throw

The same program will serve for the discus thrower, with the addition of a lateral raise exercise, lying, three sets of

10 repetitions. Fortune Gordien also used the lateral raise, standing, for added deltoid strength, the rise-on-toes for calf spring, and a "dumbbell discus throw" movement. He would wind up for the throw and go through the acceleration of turning to bring the weight up to shoulder level. Immediately after following a weight-training program (which he continued during early throwing practice days), Gordien set a world record of 194-6.

Hammer Throw

For the hammer thrower, the shot-putters' routine will again prove basically sound, but additional work should be included to develop strength over short-range leg extension and in the trapezius. Three sets of at least three (attempting to do five) cleans are invaluable power builders. This is not the competitive-style clean of the weight-lifter, but an all-the-way-up pull from floor to shoulders without moving the feet, and with only slight knee dip to receive the weight at the chest. The cleans should be started with the erect crouch. The upright rowing exercise, working up from eight to 12 repetitions and adding weight, is another good movement for the hammer thrower.

Bob Backus, who set records in the 35- and 56-pound weight throws, emphasized heavy squats, cleans, and supine presses in his weight-training program. He also did two sets of shoulder-shrugging movements, using 380 pounds for 10 repetitions, and heavy partial squats (approximately one-quarter knee dip) with 600 pounds on his shoulders for three sets of 10 repetitions.

Javelin Throw

1. Clean and press, 10 repetitions, light weight.
2. Alternate press, dumbbells; 10 repetitions each arm, two sets (pressing with speed).
3. Squat, five repetitions, four sets.
4. Pullover, 10 repetitions after each set of squats (using light weight).
5. Sit-up with weight behind head, twisting to touch elbows to opposite knees, alternately. If possible, the javelin thrower should do sit-ups with his legs supported only to the buttocks, so his torso can back-bend slightly at the low point.
6. Supine press, five repetitions, four sets.
7. Straight-arm lateral raise, 10 repetitions.
8. Throwing motion using pulley weight, 10 to 20 "throws." A section of javelin handle, with grip binding, can be attached to the pulley rope, or the regular pulley handle can be held in the hand.
9. Chinning or rope-climbing.

An exercise suggested by Dr. McCloy,* shrugging forward while lying supine with a barbell at straight arms over the chest, should be used by shot, discus, and javelin men whenever possible. McCloy says that exercise develops the serratus anterior muscle, which is important in throwing due to its function of pulling the scapula forward. Because the action is over a very short range, the exercise can easily be practiced three sets of 10 repetitions without fatigue, even though heavy weights are used. McCloy believes this exercise can increase distance in the discus throw by as much as 15 feet.

---

* Dr. Charles H. McCloy, Professor of Physical Education at the State University of Iowa.

It is difficult to say which of the weight-training movements are most valuable for participants in the sports covered in this chapter, but the exercises that appear in every schedule are the clean, press, and squat. It is possible to develop the abdominal muscles by sit-ups and leg-raises without weight (though more strength is acquired through using resistance) and the arms and upper back by chinning. The triceps and pectorals will respond to dipping (on parallel bars and in the "pushup") but not to the extent that they will with more than the body's weight. For complete development of shoulder and arm strength, however, there is no better exercise than the overhead press with barbell or dumbbells. No exercise is better than the squat with barbell on shoulders to develop sheer strength in the legs. No other form of exercise remotely approaches lifting a barbell from the floor for development of the powerful muscles of the lower back. For these reasons, the clean, press, and squat with barbell should be practiced to some degree by every athlete who wants to give his best possible performance.

Index

A

Abilene Christian College, 2
Arch-flyaway, 103

B

Babka, Rink, 160
Backus, Bob, 110, 190
Bailey, Jim, 60
Bannister, Roger, 48
Baton passing, 84, 90, 91
Bausch, Jim, 52
Beatty, Jim, 53
Bell, Greg, 128, 129, 130, 133, 134
Blair, Cliff, 110
Blind pass, 86, 88
Blocks (*See* Sprints)
Body, building (*See also* Weight, lifting), 124
Bonthron, Bill, 56
Boston, Ralph, 130, 133
Boston University, 109, 110, 112, 121
Bowden, Don, 52, 53, 60, 62, 64
Bragg, Don, 96
Bresnahan, George T., 179, 184
Broad jump, 127-138
  form in the air, 132
  hitch kick, 132, 134
  injuries, 136
  knee-tuck style, 132
  landing, 133
  meet, before the, 137
  physical requirements, 129
  run, the, 131
  "running in air," 132
  selecting, 130

Broad jump (*Cont.*):
  straight-away jump, 132
  styles, 132
  "the take-off," 131
  training, 136
  warming up, 136
  weight, lifting, 136
  workouts, 136
  training, 193
Burleson, Dyrol, 53

C

Calhoun, Lee, 13, 68
Calisthenics, 15, 124, 154, 190
Campbell, Milt, 128
Championship Technique in Track and Field, 140
Chandler, Otis, 190, 194
Circle positions, 143-147
Cochran, Dick, 160
Collymore, Ed, 26
Connolly, Harold, 110
Cooper, John M., 129
Courtney, Tom, 39, 48
Cretzmeyer, Francis X., 171, 172, 179, 181, 184
Cromwell, Dean, 140
Cross-Country, 171-184
  fartlek training, 44, 176, 179
  form, 173
  "Four-Minute Mile," 178
  health and, 183
  injuries, 183
  meet, before the, 179
  physical requirements, 173
  running form, 173
  stride, 174